The Futures Effect

The Futures Effect

Change Your Story, Change Y'our Future!

Tom Meyers

This book or any portion thereof is subject to international copyright and may not be copied in any way without the prior written permission of the publisher.

ISBN 9789403683508

The author of this book does not dispense medical advice or prescribe the use of any technique as a form of treatment for physical, emotional, or medical problems without the advice of a physician, either directly or indirectly. The intent of the author is only to offer information of a general nature to help you in your quest for physical, emotional and spiritual wellbeing.

Words fine-tuned by Graham Buik www.idisambiguate.com

Cover design © 2023 by MaryDes Designs Ltd

Copyright © 2023 Tom Meyers

After today, you'll never be the same again.

TESTIMONIALS

Tom Meyers, in his new book *The Futures Effect*, provides an engaging and highly practical approach to transforming your consciousness and your way of life.

Written in a clear, direct, and easily understandable style, Meyers' book highlights the critical importance of understanding and guiding your life from the perspective of your envisioned future. Instead of following the habits and mindsets of the past, the key to a better life is to become more conscious of the future and its possibilities and opportunities—to infuse the future into the present. For Meyers, the future should become a way of life.

The Futures Effect examines the essentials of personal empowerment and taking a proactive, rather than reactive stance toward life's challenges.

Embracing the concept of self-directed purposeful evolution—we have the power to personally evolve ourselves—Meyers discusses how to successfully prepare for the stress-provoking rapid changes of modern life, creating a "resilient future," and how to envisage a "future self" to serve as a guiding light for navigating and understanding the present.

Meyers addresses human emotions and feelings, decision-making and planning, knowledge and thinking, and purpose, self-narratives, and self-identity in outlining his futurist philosophy.

Filled with illuminating examples from his own personal history and experiences—of difficulties and successes and insights—Meyers' *The Futures Effect* is an enthusiastic and constructive roadmap for heightening one's future consciousness and re-energizing one's life.

Thomas Lombardo, Ph.D.

Director of the *Center for Future Consciousness*

Executive Board Member and Fellow of the *World Futures Studies Federation*

Author of *Future Consciousness: The Path to Purposeful Evolution, Essays on the Future of Psychology and Consciousness*, and numerous other books and publications

As an osteopath and an autodidact futurist, Tom links the most important skills from futures thinking to learn how to feel with your whole being.

His vision is not so much about shaping your vision about the future; it's about shaping your feelings about the future and using that as an instrument to choose directions. It is not a book that is made to be read at one time. It reads like it is simple, but it is not. It's a book that you should read chapter by chapter and think through and let the content make sense for you before passing on to the next chapter. You need to take time to digest.

In his writing, Tom takes you by the hand. Sometimes the text seems to repeat but then it comes to another point for which you still had to go back to what was told before. He teaches us personal futures thinking through his own experiences and underpins them with lots of research from other futurists, (mental) health experts, philosophers, and scientists.

My greatest learning from the book is that a lot of things are uncertain but there are also a lot of things you can count on. I love the insight that "…certain feelings I longed for were constant in life, like feeling content, fulfilled and healthy… I knew I would not always experience those things, but I would always be striving for them".

Working with Tom on GREAT futures is not about knowing; his futures effect is about wisdom with all your body, mind and soul.

Linda Hofman MSc.
Senior lecturer & futures researcher, Fontys Academy for Creative Industries

This book is all about inspiring you to think constructively about your future. By providing a straightforward and useful framework based on unwavering principles, it fosters the development of a guiding narrative for the future, for one's life.

By using that framework, we can define and design a preferred scenario of the future that is better than one left up to chance. Everyone can easily follow the steps suggested by the book to progress, live a meaningful life, and assure a "GREAT" future in this fast changing and challenging world. It teaches us how to analyse, develop, and pursue our preferred plans using language that is simple to read and understand.

The clever use of "Y'our" rather than "Your" by the author serves to remind us that our choices, decisions, and actions influence more than just our own lives. We must thus construct our future based on that awareness to be responsible people who care about the future.

For readers at all educational levels who want to live a purposeful life in our volatile, uncertain, complex, and ambiguous (VUCA) environment, this book is highly helpful.

Alireza Hejazi, Ph.D.

Analyst for Leadership and Futures Studies and author of a.o. *Responsible Foresight* and *Becoming A Professional Futurist*

CONTENTS

Preface	**15**
Introduction	**19**
Envisaging your future self	20
The future as a way of life	23
The future is y'our future	26
Futurizing yourself is adopting a futures mindset	29
The benefits for y'our health and wellbeing	31
Think and act like y'our future depends on it	35
A chance of a lifetime	38
Living for tomorrow is living for today	40
The Futures Effect	42
Chapter 1: What, The Future?!	**47**
What to do about the future	48
Evolving on purpose	52
Your choices today determine y'our tomorrow	55
Change your story to change y'our future	58
The future is not what it used to be	62
The power of futures thinking	66
The proactive approach	71
It's only too late if you don't start	74
WTF?! Knowledge is power	76
The future is here – get used to it	81
A GREAT future becomes a GREAT life	84
Chapter 2: A Good Future	**89**
What does a good future feel like?	90
What do you need to have a good life?	96
How do you create a good future?	101
One step, two steps, three – the future is in me	105
Let the future pull you forward	110
Built for a purpose	115

When the future comes knocking at your door	118
The future of possibilities	126
Take an overview perspective	130

Chapter 3: A Resilient Future — 133

Best wishes for your future	134
The push and pull of the future	139
Say hi to the primordial futurist	143
But what is stress–resilience?	158
Not all challenges are signs to change	164
The future as a milestone	169
Rehearse your future	171
We all need something to look forward to in life	175
Rewiring the brain for the future	177
Making your future self your best friend	183
Developing a resilient future	184
Everything that can be automated will be automated	188
Design your life on purpose	190

Chapter 4: An Evolvable Future — 197

Connecting the dots	198
The evolving sense of self	203
Next steps	206
Repeating patterns	209
Catching opportunities	213
Making decisions that work for you	218
As you see y'our future, so you act. As you act, …	225
Can we evolve on purpose?	230
Avoid distractions and stay focused	234
Embracing y'our evolvable future	236
Being a pragmatic futurist	242
How to feel about the future	249
The Strange Order of Things	252

Chapter 5: An Actionable Future — 255

Empowerment	256
Exploring y'our future	261
Principles guide behaviour	264
Time is key to understanding y'our evolution	271
Don't be scared – be prepared for the future	277
The future matters	283
The future reimagined	287
Chapter 6: A Transcendent Future	**289**
Being a good ancestor	290
Chapter 7: Your Future Self	**295**
Embracing your future self	296
Future self-continuity	300
Forewarned is forearmed	303
Rewire yourself for the future	306
Afterword	**311**
Futurize Yourself	312
Addendum	**320**
Resources	**325**
References	**326**

The Futures Effect

PREFACE

What do you want the future to be like?

What do you aspire to achieve, feel, create and be remembered for?

Don't answer immediately, even if you know the answer.

For now, just take a deep breath, close your eyes and step inside yourself. Slowly breathe in and out, feel within and connect with your inner being.

How do you feel? Don't think, just observe.

Now, imagine you are travelling to the future – to your last day on Earth – and look back. With an overview perspective, look at yourself – your life – like an astronaut would look at the Earth when they arrive in an orbit around our planet for the first time. Look back on your life with the same awe and connection astronauts feel when they see the Earth from this cosmic perspective. Look back at what has come and gone but also your outlook on life, your desires and aspirations. Do this without judgement but with a thankful, open heart, an open mind and curiosity.

You are now a time-travelling astronaut who is looking back from the future. Observe – don't judge or use words to describe what you see. Let the feelings flow in and out at the rhythm of your breath, and let the images that emerge unfold like a film in front of your mind's eye. Feel and observe with wonder and awe all the steps you took, the decisions and choices you made and the actions you took, and all the experiences and learnings of the years that have brought you to this, your final day on Earth.

How do you feel viewing yourself from this future perspective?

Whatever feelings come rolling over you, acknowledge them, be grateful, and say "Thank you". Don't let yourself be overwhelmed by the feelings or realisations, but let them help you raise your awareness.

Keep your eyes closed for a moment longer. With your mind's eye, keep looking back – but now, expand your awareness. Expand your field of vision and start seeing around you. You are not alone. You are of one with more than 8 billion souls. Souls that are having the same experience as you and, like you, are travelling on Spaceship Earth that is moving at a speed of 107,000 kilometres per hour around the Sun.

You are, of one, moving together in a fast-changing and ever more complex world, as you can see from this perspective. Zoom in and you'll see that you are of one, connected through decisions, choices, actions and more.

Observe and see how what you say or do influences others and how others, in turn, influence the many and shape your behaviour, as you are one. Hold on to that insight.

Now, refocus your awareness back to you and ask yourself: "If this was indeed my last day on Earth, am I content and fulfilled with what I have achieved? Was I good to myself, my health and wellbeing? Was I able to adapt and self-manage myself in what has become a fast-changing world? Was my life meaningful? Did I become a better person? And now, leaving this world, am I leaving it a better place than it was when I entered it? Will I be considered a good ancestor?"

What say you?

Would others agree with your conclusions? Or…

It's time to go back, until we meet again.

But before you go, tell me: What do you want your future to be like? Or, as I like to put it: What "the future" do you want?

It is time…

Be good to you and y'our future, always.

And then, I wake up.

The Futures Effect

Introduction

It's up to you to change your story, to change y'our future.

Tom Meyers

Envisaging your future self

The future is the act of creation and we are all participating in it.

Thomas Lombardo

Have you ever considered or taken the time to think about your future self? I mean, really taken the time to reflect about who you ideally would like to be, how you want to feel, what your ideal day would look like?

What "the future" do you want 10, 20 or more years from now? When I was asked to envisage my future self and describe a perfect day 10 years into the future – that was more than 20 years ago now – I was really taken aback and even a bit dismissive about what I was being asked to do.

What was the point of thinking about the future when my business was failing and I along with it? How was it possible to imagine beauty when there was nothing but darkness all around? How was it possible to hypothetically think of a bright future in 10 or more years' time, when I wanted change today? My situation was dire, and it needed to be fixed now! Depressed and wallowing in self-pity, it felt a preposterous task and a waste of time to think about the future while faced with so many problems in the here and now.

However, luckily, I did as I was asked. Now, with hindsight, I know that contemplating what the future I wanted and conceiving a preferred future was exactly what I needed and the best strategy to pull myself out of my misery.

Who would have thought that what seemed preposterous, even impossible, would become the key to the mindshift I needed in my time of crisis? I didn't. Nor did I imagine that it would become the starting point for what I so much longed for – to feel content, fulfilled and healthy. The primary feelings that lie at the basis of health and wellbeing.

But not only that: every aspect of my life has benefited from "futurizing" myself, as I've come to refer to the process of designing and living one's life on purpose. A process and mindset where, instead of leaving life and your future up to chance, you design the future you want based on self-defined unwavering principles and proactively pull it towards you through the decisions and choices you make and the actions you take.

> In this book, I'm introducing two new words: **"y'our"** and **"y'ourself"**.
>
> **"Y'our"** is an amalgam of "your" and "our", and **"y'ourself"** is the combination of "yourself" and "ourself". ("Ourself" is different from "ourselves" and refers to people in general rather than a definite group of people.)
>
> As we focus on the future, I'm convinced it is vital for us to understand that we are not alone, never were and never will be, and that our decisions, choices and actions have an impact on others and vice versa.
>
> In many ways, this accords with the Golden Rule, the principle of treating others as one wants to be treated – but what I want to emphasise here is the importance of being mindful that, whatever you do, your decisions, choices and actions are going to have an effect on others.
>
> So, when you see "y'our" and "y'ourself" used in this book, I hope this will help you (= you, the reader as an individual!) to keep this important aspect in mind.

So I'd like to ask you: What sort of future are you creating for y'ourself? Are you actively creating the future? Or do you face it day by day, leave it up to chance, and find yourself being pushed towards an unknown destiny?

Contrary to what you might think, you can have a say in what kind of future will ensue by choosing a future before a future is chosen for you. **You can have a say, as every decision and choice you make – every action you take – steers the course of y'our future.**

The future as a way of life

If you don't have a strategy, you're part of someone else's strategy.

Alvin Toffler

Today, we are living in a fast-changing and ever more complex and ambiguous world. A world that is trying to cope with and navigate the COVID-19 pandemic and the devastating effects of climate change. At the same time, every aspect of our life is being influenced by automation, robotisation, datafication and so many other changes and challenges due to technological advances that have outpaced our own evolution.

In other words, we are living in a time with many seemingly uncontrollable changes and challenges which can induce a feeling of uncertainty and insecurity. This often leads to stress, anxiety and indecision due to fear of making the wrong choices.

Change itself is changing, and it is doing so very rapidly. How you handle this is key to y'our health and wellbeing – even y'our existence. Change is inevitable, and rebelling against it will not change anything but will only make it worse for you in the long run. However, it is also not enough to just accept that everything changes or that change is a constant. You need to embrace change and change yourself or, as I prefer to say, evolve with it on purpose.

As an osteopath and body-centred stress coach, I often think about the question of how we will cope with all these changes. What we need and what you can do to evolve on purpose to stay healthy in body, mind and spirit in this fast-changing world. There is so much at stake.

I know it is normal for us, for organisations and policymakers alike, to concentrate on the immediate threat(s) we are facing. It is normal to react, in the present, to the changes which have already occurred and which are affecting us now. When faced with a fire, you have to react and tackle it straight away in order to safeguard yourself and others.

However, preventing a fire is better, and this requires proactivity, the conscious decisions where you work out possible scenarios and take action to prevent them from occurring. At the same time, thinking about scenarios on how to handle a fire is also crucial for being able to react better when a fire actually breaks out.

We invest too little time thinking about scenarios for the future. Rarely do we ask what the future we want and/or how we will cope with the multitude of changes ahead. Rarely do we want to see too far ahead; this is often due to fear, as thinking about the future can be very scary. We'd rather hide behind the premise "what will be will be…". So we're inclined to refuse to think about unpleasant facts, and we prefer to wait and see.

This kind of reactive thinking strategy has become as problematic as not having a strategy at all. It makes me think of the words of American polymath Benjamin Franklin (1706–1790): "If you fail to plan, you are planning to fail!"

At the moment, when it comes to the future it's as if we are walking across a busy street aimlessly and without first looking left or right to see if there is any oncoming danger. We are not even looking ahead.

Then we're surprised when we're in the middle of the street and faced with an oncoming car.

In many ways, a part of futurizing yourself is like crossing a busy street. First, you need to decide where you want to be on purpose. Then, before you make any decisions or choices or take any action, you look ahead and anticipate possible challenges or obstacles you will need to deal with or overcome. Only then do you make your way and navigate the road ahead towards your preferred future. This works most of the time, but now and then something unexpected happens, as no plan is perfect and the future is and remains unpredictable. Thus, you can still find yourself in the path of an unexpected trend or event that wasn't on your radar and to which you need to react to. However, with the future as your ally, you'll know how to react to any unexpected events.

> "The future hasn't arrived yet. Do your best to try to shape it in the present moment, but always remember some things are just out of our control, and that's fine."
>
> Robert Washington

Unexpected events will always happen, but when you futurize yourself you will always have a strategy to fall back on.

The future is y'our future

Today, neither past nor present but the future has become the key to y'our existence.

Tom Meyers

The future is y'our future, and the likelihood that the future will become a continuous distressing battle against the odds is significantly increased if you and we leave it all up to chance. Already today, most of the significant problems we battle against exist because we left things to chance, didn't think ahead about the consequences, or left it up to others to decide.

> Be aware that the future arrives more slowly than you think and more quickly than you can imagine. However, even though we are switched-on all the time to the point of distraction, we are not so switched-on when it comes to seeing what is in plain sight.

Today, in the midst of turmoil, where short-term pressures are up against medium and long-term uncertainties, humanity is at a precipice and its future is at stake (Stansberry et al. 2019).

Today, we are living in what is considered by the United Nations as "The Decade of Action" (2020–2030). We have 10 years to reinvent ourselves and find sustainable solutions to all the world's biggest challenges – ranging from poverty and gender to climate change, inequality and closing the finance gap.

We have to reinvent ourselves, which isn't easy, but we can

make it a lot easier when we learn to use our mental time-travelling potential to look up and ahead and envisage the reality of the catastrophe that awaits if we don't do anything.

> "The Earth is at a tipping point and we face a stark choice: either we continue as we are and irreparably damage our planet, or we remember our unique power as human beings and our continual ability to lead, innovate and problem-solve. People can achieve great things. The next ten years present us with one of our greatest tests – a decade of action to repair the Earth."
>
> **Prince William, The Earthshot Prize, 2019**

Yesterday, while watching the film *Don't Look Up*, I also watched – by coincidence (or not) – an extract from the programme *28 minutes* on Arte (6 January 2022). In the extract, journalist Salomé Saqué tries to warn the panel and audience about the climate catastrophe. The reaction of the panel was… laughter and ridicule. It was like a scene straight out of the film.

The problem is so big and overwhelming that I think we don't want to see it and would rather bury our heads in the sand or laugh it off, hope for the best and believe it won't happen so quickly. But deep down, we know the truth. Deep down, you know.

It's a classic trap that the future arrives more slowly than we think and more quickly than we can imagine. Just look around and you'll see that the future is already here.

The question now is: how do you secure y'our future and the future of the future? How do you overcome your fear and possible short-sightedness?

> **The future of the future**
>
> The events that will or are likely to happen in time to come are changing in the time that is (as yet) still to come.

You overcome it by designing y'our future on purpose, and to pull y'our future towards you through the decisions and choices you make and the actions you take. You overcome it one step at a time with a GREAT future for yourself and humankind in mind.

(Over the next few pages, I will explain exactly what I mean by **"a GREAT future"**.) Your steps, even small ones, matter, in the bigger scheme of things.

To quote the words of Queen Elizabeth II spoken in a video message for the 26th United Nations Climate Change Conference (Glasgow) evening reception (1 November 2021): "Of course, the benefits of such actions will not be there to enjoy for all of us here today: none of us will live forever. But we are doing this not for ourselves but for our children and our children's children, and those who will follow in their footsteps."

Futurizing yourself is adopting a futures mindset

You cannot create the future using the old strategy tools ... The big challenge in creating the future is not predicting the future; instead the goal is to try to imagine a future that is plausible, that you can create.

Charles Handy

It's time to learn from y'our past but think back from y'our future history that you envisage and create on purpose. It's time to stop being too focused on the now, and adopt a new mindset that looks to the future in a bid to overcome y'our fears. It's time to create a GREAT future, a future in a way that best suits and assures y'our health and wellbeing and the wellbeing of our planet on which we depend.

In a GREAT future, we have a common cause and the necessary anchor points to create the stability and clarity we need to overcome our fears. A GREAT future is where we become the best version of ourselves and where, to quote Douglas Rushkoff, author of *Team Human*, "We can be fully human without being in complete control of our world."

A GREAT future, i.e., a GREAT life, requires an open mind and some thought. It's time to start living on purpose. When you live on purpose, you're adding meaning into your life and moving in a preferred direction. It's time to believe that y'our individual actions matter. It's time that you act like y'our future and the future of the future depends on it. Because it does.

We can cope with and navigate the global changes and challenges that lie ahead by using the future. You can drive the changes needed to pull y'ourself out of this crisis facing humanity before it is too late. I know you can, because I have experienced not only how futurizing myself has changed me but also how its benefits have rippled through my environment.

I'm not saying futurizing yourself is the solution to all y'our problems. However, I do believe that, at the core, futurizing yourself is an important contribution to the change in mindset that is needed to start the "Great Reset" needed to tackle some of the biggest personal and global challenges we are facing.

The future is a collective endeavour, for everybody, by everyone. The future needs you. In these unsettling times, with everything changing so rapidly and so extensively, there is a great need to find stability and clarity, something to hold on to while everything changes.

The benefits for y'our health and wellbeing

Once your future self becomes alive in your mind, you may find it much easier to make the small personal sacrifices that are essential to preserve your wellbeing. And in the years ahead, you'll thank yourself for that forethought.

David Robson

Futurizing yourself is something that everyone can do and benefit from. However, what will be different for each individual is where you start the process of defining y'our future on purpose and proactively incorporate futures thinking into your decisions, choices and actions to "change forward" and create a GREAT future for y'ourself.

It depends on where you find yourself, the stage of life you are in, the baggage that you are carrying along and/or whether or not other essential needs are met. There are 8 billion different starting points, so to speak.

> **Futurize Yourself**
>
> Futurizing yourself is living your life on purpose. Instead of leaving your life and the future up to chance, you use images of your preferred future as a starting point to change your behaviour in the present.
>
> It is a conscious process and mindset where you proactively incorporate futures thinking into your present-moment decisions, choices and actions that are consistent with the future you want, and it contributes to better, more meaningful living and a GREAT future for y'ourself.
>
> This process is based on a narrative for your future that you have taken the time to envisage and develop by means of three steps.

> The first step starts with creating a new narrative for the past when you have, for example, limiting beliefs about yourself and/or about the way the world works.
>
> The second step is to uncover and define your potential (i.e., the talents you were born with) and in addition define how you want to feel (innate expression of wellbeing) on any given day and your aspirations (hopes for the future) that don't change over time (unwavering principles).
>
> The third step is to create a narrative for your preferred future based on steps one and two. A narrative that is agile enough to cope with changes including your personal evolution, changing demands of the world of work, the changing environment, megashifts and megatrends.

My own three-step process started at a time when life had become meaningless and a never-ending uphill battle. Tired of fighting against the odds and emotionally drained, I remember waking up one morning in my cold, damp bedroom thinking: "If this is what life is about, this continuous struggle to survive, I don't want it." But what did I want?

That said, I am still futurizing myself. It is an ongoing process. The approach is very different now than when I started 22 years ago, but the essence and what the future I want haven't changed.

What I want is what I believe you and we all want. It is something we have in common, no matter at what stage of life you find yourself. What you/we want at y'our most intrinsic level is to feel content, fulfilled and healthy, and what you/we want to have is a future that is **G**ood, **R**esilient, **E**volvable, **A**ctionable and **T**ranscendent, i.e., **a GREAT future**.

Introduction

Why do you/we want this? Because we all want to flourish in the flow of evolution and thrive in this ever-evolving, fast-changing world. We want to **flourish** – to grow or develop in a healthy way the non-material part of us that goes beyond the confines of simple happiness or wellbeing. We also want to **thrive** – and by that, I mean to succeed in material terms.

> I wish I had come up with the words "flourishing in the flow of evolution". However, all praise goes to futurist, psychologist, educator, philosopher and author of *Future Consciousness – The Path to Purposeful Evolution*, Thomas Lombardo. A book that speaks to my heart which addresses "How to create a good future by developing a core set of character virtues, most notably and centrally wisdom."

We want this because this is what we innately strive for. Life needs a sense, a direction in which we can excel and expand our feeling of belonging and wholeness. Just imagine a GREAT future – a life where you feel content, fulfilled and healthy, while making a meaningful impact on the lives of others by growing into the best version of yourself in a purposeful way.

Do you want this?

Maybe you've never looked at your life or your future from this perspective before. If so, let me encourage you to give it a go. I think you will be pleasantly surprised!

And while it makes sense that focusing on the moment can improve your wellbeing, so can futurizing yourself. Because futurizing yourself makes you more willing to look after yourself. It also gives your life a direction, makes it more meaningful, makes you more responsible for your present-day behaviour, and makes making decisions and choices – and life in general – easier. Because creating and nurturing a vivid sense of your future self will increase the extent you feel more continuity between your present and your future self (future self-continuity), and the more likely it is that you will make decisions, make choices and take actions with your future self in mind.

Future self-continuity

Future self-continuity is the extent that people feel more continuity between their present and future selves, resulting in them being more likely to make decisions with the future self in mind.

"Focusing on one's connection to the future self may help one realize the long road of repeated healthy decisions to improve long-term health, and perhaps this process would be further facilitated by shifting priorities, yielding a trajectory of self-reinforcing positive behaviors. Acting today for health benefits that may not be seen until far in the future may be easier to do when recognizing one's connection to that future, specifically to one's future self."

(Rutchick et al. 2018)

Introduction

Think and act like y'our future depends on it

The past has passed. The present happens too fast. Yet, futures are our only chance to change, to improve and to generate opportunities that best suits you, with yourself, your surroundings and with others.

Alethia Montero

You are far more remarkable than you think. "There has never been a you before, and there will never be a you again" (Dustin Hoffman). You are unique, and y'our future needs you. It is up to you to choose how you want to feel… and shape your reality. You have the power over your future history – to change the world and make it a better place – by changing yourself.

But as the past has already come and gone and the present is happening too fast, then the only direction from which you can instigate the changes needed to make a difference is the future. "Even though the future seems far away, it is actually beginning right now" (Mattie Stepanek) – and "What you do today can improve all your tomorrows" (Ralph Marston). Believe in yourself, believe in your future – because, "If there is hope in the future, there is literally power in the present" (Zig Ziglar).

"Don't be scared – be prepared for the future" (Sylvia Gallusser). Contemplate what the future will bring or what you would like to see, feel, or avoid in the future. This requires a change from today's more predominant "focus on the present" mindset. To be mindful of the present of y'our current environment is a strategy that doesn't prepare you for what is to come.

In his book *Future Consciousness*, Tom Lombardo writes that flourishing within the human condition requires a purposeful future focus. Furthermore, he writes that it is unquestionably the case that living in the relative present is the fundamental cause behind many of our most significant problems, including global warming. Some scientists like Rutchick et al. (2018) also see many of our current health challenges as problems of prioritising present (immediate gratification) over future (long-term) benefits.

Y'our mind, based on millions of years of evolution, is not constructed to live in the present. To evolve, there needs to be a purpose, a direction or, in other words, a future focus. It is the nature of the conscious human mind that you act with purpose and perceive with anticipation.

Dr Bob Johansen (2020), a futurist with the Institute for the Future (IFTF), explains that what you need in the middle of a crisis is the North Star that gives you clarity. It's often easier to look 10 years ahead than to look one or two years ahead, especially in a crisis. What the brain wants is certainty – and when the immediate future is difficult to predict, as it is today, we can reach greater clarity by thinking long term.

What is your North Star? What the future do you want?

The future – y'our future – doesn't exist, but it is given shape by every decision and choice you make and the actions you take. Just look at how your behaviour and life changes when you make short-term or medium-term plans like planning your weekend, or your next holiday. When you entered higher education or started a hobby, you wanted the future to be something, and you aligned yourself to that.

Today, the future – y'our future – is at stake. We suppress the thought, but if you dare to think about it, you know it is so. However, denying it doesn't make it go away.

Futurizing yourself is living from a futures perspective. It creates the needed structure to overcome many of our current problems which, in many ways, are related to a conflict in evolution. Our evolution is too slow to cope with the fast-changing world we have created, so it is time to come to its aid. Not by becoming technology, but by the power of y'our imagination that you can put to good use.

A chance of a lifetime

Your life and behaviour immediately shift when you begin imagining a different future and stridently striving for it.

Benjamin P. Hardy

In these unsettling times, with everything changing so rapidly and so extensively, there is a great need to find stability and clarity – something to hold on to while everything changes.

Futurizing yourself offers you the mental structure to think about the future and build the future starting today. Are you ready?

Are you ready to build a GREAT future? A future that is Good – a future where you flourish and thrive, where you are Resilient and feel that you are Evolving into the best version of yourself, where your Actions matter and where future generations will thank you for having Transcended yourself?

I know that, when we look at our immediate problems, thinking about the bigger and long-term picture might seem pointless. I've been there, done that, got the T-shirt! But now I know better. The future is y'our future, and it's better to "change before you have to" (Jack Welch).

And, if you – if we – want a GREAT future, to feel content, fulfilled and healthy in this fast-changing and challenging world, a world where COVID-19, new emerging technologies and other global crises like climate change are challenging every aspect of y'our life, including y'our very survival, the future is the best place to start.

Yes, you can turn a blind eye to y'our future ("Que Sera, Sera") – and leave it all to chance, or you can decide to futurize yourself and envisage the future you want to create and evolve into, and then systematically and deliberately align your decisions, choices and actions to the future you want.

Because the good thing about the future – unlike the past – is that it is always in the making. The GREAT future lies in your decisions, choices and actions. For now…

But y'our time is running out.

As I mentioned earlier, I'm concerned about y'our future and especially the lack of consideration that is being given to how we – you, me and humanity at large – will cope with all the changes and challenges that lie ahead and which will, without a doubt, increase the already out-of-control levels of stress.

Stress is a survival response that is experienced when demands outweigh y'our resources. When left unmanaged, it leads to musculoskeletal, cardiovascular, respiratory and immune problems. Stress also adds to anxiety and depression, mood changes, memory problems and changes in time perception.

As changes and challenges increase, so too will stress levels and therefore also all the biopsychosocial and spiritual health problems that are related to and made worse by stress. I can already see in my practice how this is playing out – and more change is coming.

It is forecast that the next 10 years will bring more changes than the past 100 years! I hope you understand why I am concerned. How will we cope with all these changes and prevent stress from further becoming a hazard to our health and wellbeing and our future?

The solution is very simple: we cannot solve our problems with the same thinking we used when we created them.

The Futures Effect

Living for tomorrow is living for today

The reality we will experience tomorrow is in part a product of the mindsets we hold today.

Alia Crum

For thousands of years, focusing on present or imminent danger has helped us to survive and deal with physical threats. But now that our environment is evolving faster than we are and the threats to our existence have changed, fight or flight doesn't work any more. On the contrary: the fight or flight – i.e., stress – response itself has become a source of stress.

So, if nature is too slow, what can we do to give it a helping hand? Can it be done without becoming technology, without choosing the transhumanist path? Yes! If present thinking has got us here, what will get us out of here is a futures thinking mindset. A mindset where the future is not a continuation of the past but where the past is seen as a teacher, and where a GREAT future, designed on purpose, guides our decisions, choices and actions in the present and makes us feel content, fulfilled and healthy.

We all need to start exploring the future to help us evolve on purpose. While the past and present will undoubtedly shape the future to some degree, we need to create scenarios for the future 10, 20 and more years from now, imagine what we want and don't want, and with those images in mind, steer the course of our future through our decisions, choices and actions.

With the future in mind, determination and volition, we can steer the course of our future and prepare ourselves to get a better grip on the future. A grip is needed to navigate the changes ahead. We cannot wait for others to decide or to do what lies within our power.

In other words, you can proactively choose a future before a future is chosen for you. I call that process "futurizing yourself": proactively and on purpose incorporating futures thinking into your present-moment decisions, choices and actions that are consistent with scenarios of your preferred future – a process that contributes to better, more meaningful living and a GREAT future for y'ourself.

This means consciously spending time informing yourself – defining a narrative for your past, finding your potential, features of wellbeing and aspirations – and creating scenarios for the future. It means envisaging how our lives, jobs, environment – what you and we want or don't want – will be influenced by y'our personal evolution, changing demands of the world of work, the changing environment, megashifts and megatrends.

It means using these scenarios as a tool to make better plans and direct your decisions, choices and actions today. BUT: a GREAT future is never lived alone. What you think, say, decide, choose or do, every step you take and every move you make influences other people who, in turn, will influence others. It's something we're not always aware of, but that doesn't make it less true. Thus, although futurizing yourself is done for and by you, always keep in mind that your decisions, choices and actions affect others.

The Futures Effect

If you get really good at investing your energy into your future in the present moment, and thus your body starts following your mind to that future, wouldn't you agree when you start seeing all those wonderful synchronicities, coincidences, and serendipities in your life that you're going to keep doing it? And wouldn't you also agree that you're going to become more aware of your challenges, conditions, and tests when they are happening?

Dr Joe Dispenza

You are the key to y'our future. You have far more agency over y'our future and the future of the future than you imagine. However, most likely you have neglected the future or not used its potential to y'our advantage. But now that the world is evolving faster than we are, using the future – or, in other words, futurizing yourself – has become key to making a difference in all aspects of life.

For example, how can futurizing yourself be useful for y'our health and wellbeing?

On a global scale, the future of y'our health and wellbeing depends on keeping the average annual global temperature from rising more than 1.5 degrees Celsius above pre-industrial levels. If you want to avoid the most catastrophic and long-term effects of climate change like widespread famine, to limit sea level rise to a few feet, prevent economic and financial collapse, and avert war in your lifetime or that of your children, then you will need to make sure you align your decisions, choices and actions with a future that prevents these scenarios from becoming a reality.

On a personal level, your health and wellbeing also depend on how fulfilling your life is. So ask yourself: how happy are you doing what you are doing today? If you are not happy, then this will affect how you feel, your health and wellbeing. Think about it.

Maybe the following two observations can help you think about it further: "Most of us live two lives! The first one is the life we actually live; the second is the imagined life where we achieve all the success we dream about. Some build a bridge between these two lives" (Vlad Zachary); "A human being is not one in pursuit of happiness but rather in search of a reason to become happy, last but not least, through actualising the potential meaning inherent and dormant in a given situation" (Viktor Frankl).

Maybe you are a little sceptical, or feeling burdened by the past. If so, I'd like to share with you one more quote, attributed to Ziad K. Abdelnour: "Just because the past didn't turn out like you wanted it to, doesn't mean the future can't be better than you ever imagined."

The future depends on many other factors, including megatrends and megashifts. Megatrends are defined as long-term (slow-forming) driving forces that are observable now and will most likely have significant influence on the future. An example of a megatrend is climate change. Megashifts, by contrast, are exponential shifts in human experience which are sudden in arrival, and unpredictable in outcome. These include digitisation, automation, robotisation, datafication, augmentation, virtualisation, ... These will have an impact on how you live and work – and, if you are not prepared, they will affect y'our health and wellbeing.

How? Well, as an example, let's say you are a taxi driver. What do you think the future looks like for taxi drivers or the taxi industry in general? Will a taxi driver still have a job in 5 to 10 years' time? What do you think of the likelihood that the job will be influenced by megatrends like automation or robotisation?

What about your own job, for that matter? Stop reading for a moment and take your first step in futurizing yourself by going to www.replacedbyrobot.info. Type in your job title and press Enter…

If you are a taxi driver today, you will get the following message:

> **100% Chance of Automation**
>
> **"Taxi Driver" will definitely be replaced by robots.**

So if you are a taxi driver who is not approaching retirement age and you explore your future, you will see that the probable scenario for you is: unemployment, no more job – no income, problems for your family… Which, if not addressed in time, will cause a lot of distress. Y'our health and wellbeing will suffer.

According to the World Economic Forum, one-third of all jobs are at risk of automation by 2030! Are you ready? "Everything changes, the question is, do we change with it?" (John Sellars).

Will you change with it? You'll have to if you want a GREAT future where you feel content, fulfilled and healthy.

The good news is that today is your lucky day. Because, starting from today, you can still steer the course of your future by proactively considering y'our future, create images of a preferred future, and use these images to plan and change forward. You can use the images to help you make decisions and choices, take actions and evolve on purpose – starting today – to make sure that when your job has become a profession of the past seen only in documentaries or films, you already have reskilled yourself.

You have the possibility "to understand and anticipate the future! It is even possible to influence or change the future. Not all of the future, but enough to be valuable." (The author of that statement is unknown, but it's an excellent way of putting it.) Use your mental time-travelling skills wisely, and don't wait till it's too late – for y'our future is at stake.

> **The Futures Effect**
>
> *The benefits of futurizing yourself for y'our health, wellbeing and quality of life.*
>
> *Benefits that also contribute to the mitigation of climate change, creation of a more sustainable global economy, safeguarding peace, and much more ... because you decided to futurize yourself. That is to say, you decided to adopt a futures-inclusive mindset, invest in becoming the best version of yourself, and started living proactively through integrating futures thinking into all your decisions, choices and actions on purpose.*

In these unsettling times, we need a different mindset – a futures mindset that will enable us to cope with the changes and challenges ahead, and to have what we want at the end of the day: a GREAT future – a future where you, your family, friends and future generations will flourish in the flow of evolution and thrive in this fast-changing world.

Chapter 1:
What, The Future?!

If the future is not fixed or predetermined, then more than one future must be available, and it is possible to change the future through the actions we take today.

Tom Meyers

What to do about the future

We can't predict the future. However, we can imagine it and even design it; no outcome is predetermined and, as cognitive human beings, we retain the agency to shape the world we want.

Klaus Schwab & Thierry Malleret

What "the future" do you want? What would an ideal day look like in, let's say, 10, 20 years from now? Let me ask it a different way: what don't you want the future to be like?

I'm giving you carte blanche here to come up with your ideal future, the future you wholeheartedly want to evolve into. What do you want to feel, do, see, have, experience…?

Many find it daunting to think about the future, even fear the future. More precisely, we fear the unknown that the future might bring, and we would prefer things to stay the way they are. There are neurological reasons for this, also; this fear is not without cause. The magnitude of the things we foresee in the future is mind-boggling, overwhelming and scary. So much is at stake, so much seems to be straight out of a dystopian Hollywood movie, and our brain can't grasp it. The future presents so many challenges – like climate change and the continued automation and robotisation of the workforce, to name but a few – that are threatening our continued wellbeing, if not our very existence. We seem to be fixated on a defeatist future rather than seeing the opportunities that the future presents. Thinking about the future in an unordered way overloads our system, and to protect ourselves we shut it out.

But blocking it out, fearing it or having a bleak image of the future is never going to bring you a positive future. Thinking about the future in a dystopian way is counterproductive, as it will not change the future or create the future you want. What you need is a GREAT narrative for the future so that you can evolve into the best version of yourself, preferably making the best use of the essential characteristics that make you unique and which don't change over time.

"Narratives are how we make sense of life; they provide us with a context, thanks to which we can better interpret, understand and respond to the facts we observe."
(Schwab & Malleret, 2021)

You, I, and each individual on this planet, we can have far more influence over the future than one might think. You've planned a holiday before, right? Planning for a GREAT future isn't that different. The timeframe is not six months but rather 5, 10 or more years ahead. Unlike a holiday, it will also influence not just two weeks of your life but rather life itself.

With a narrative for the future, you can also steer yourself towards a preferred future, and prevent some of the threats from getting out of hand – or at least be well prepared for them. You can do this because you have a unique human feature, the capacity for mental time travel.

Through mental time travel, you can conjure up past events as well as imagine, think about and pursue future scenarios on purpose. These unique abilities are key to futurizing yourself and designing the future you want to evolve into on purpose. Or, as Thomas Lombardo, the Director of the Center for Future

Consciousness and author of the magnificent book *Future Consciousness – The Path to Purposeful Evolution*, says: "Our most important issue in my mind with respect to the future is not developing our technologies more, is not directly dealing with economic or environmental issues. The most central important issue is evolving ourselves psychologically and consciously."

As the future doesn't exist, it is the one place you can influence and thus change. Don't like what you see the future bringing? Don't like what you imagine the future is going to be like? Want to avoid a certain scenario that you think will play out in the future? Then do something about it by futurizing yourself. Your individual actions matter in the grand scheme of things.

To change y'our future, you need to change your story, change the cornerstone of your thinking, and shape y'our future into one you want. Changing the story, changing the narrative and giving shape to y'our future starts with envisaging what you want.

What I wanted when I started to futurize myself was a life in sync, a life where I evolved, a life that made sense and made me feel content, fulfilled and healthy. There was so much conflict inside of me that I could only describe it as two wheels that were turning in opposite directions.

So, what the future do you want? How do you want to feel?

Once you have accepted you have agency over your future and a sense of what you want, you can start to think about what you need to have in your life – the essential building blocks, so to speak – to make what you want into an ongoing reality.

When I did this exercise, I had just uncovered my potential, the aptitudes I had been born with but hadn't developed (see my previous book, *Futurize Yourself – Design your life on purpose*). I had been considered good for nothing, but I reasoned that I could become good at something if I developed my newly found potential as a therapist, communicator, teacher, researcher and traveller. I also reasoned that, if I was born with this potential as part of my genetic make-up, so to speak, they had to be an integral part of what I needed for life to make sense and to be content, fulfilled and healthy. Why else would I/we each have unique aptitudes?

What is your potential, what are your talents – the building blocks for you to feel the way that you want to feel? Identify and describe them. Don't know how to identify your potential? Then get a copy of my first book and/or get help like I did. I was at a loss, and the best thing I did was to accept I needed help and to get help.

Once you have an idea of your root potential, your talents (which, by the way, doesn't change but expands throughout your life), you can create a narrative for your future, you can envisage a GREAT future 10 years from now that you'd like to shape and make into an ongoing, evolving reality. The future already exists in the form of y'our potential but we/you have to develop it.

My narrative for my future was about half a page long and was then distilled into a single sentence: "I'm a therapist with my own private practice and am invited to give workshops around the world relating to a new health approach I developed, researched and wrote a book about." A phrase that I have shortened even further to: "I'm a therapist who has developed his own approach, written a book about it and is asked to give presentations and workshops around the world."

Evolving on purpose

Your vision of where or who you want to be is the greatest asset you have. Without having a goal it's difficult to score.

Paul Arden

Designing your future on purpose doesn't make it into reality; it's what comes after that which does, and sometimes that means making difficult decisions. Decisions that go against the current mindset of living for the now and forgetting about tomorrow. To change and safeguard y'our future takes courage and determination. That's why you need a narrative. You are the story you tell yourself. Change your story and you can change y'our future.

So now, with your potential in mind, it's time for the next step – time to evolve on purpose into the image of the future you want through your decisions, choices and actions. Every day you change the future. Here and now, this is your future in the making and the future of people around you. The future isn't fixed; it is created through your decisions, choices and actions. Everything you do changes the outcome of the future. You know this, but you might have never taken the time to really stand still and reflect on this.

I had never thought about this until someone told me that I could also leave it up to chance, leave the future up to happenstance ("Que Sera, Sera") or, if I wasn't happy with my future, that I could change it if I started to take part in it.

When I think back to when I started futurizing myself, it really came down to this choice. I could keep leaving life to chance and accept whatever I was going to get, or I could take control over it by designing the future I wanted to create and then, through my decisions, choices and actions, evolve into it.

I chose the latter. This was not a sudden insight or a spur-of-the-moment decision; it was a three-step process initiated over three months. A process I also didn't come up with on my own. I had help, and now I'm here to help you. As a healer/therapist, communicator and teacher, I feel the urge within that part of my purpose is to share my experience with you.

The future is not what it used to be in this fast-paced, ever more digitised world. Already our world is being threatened by the effects of climate change, and millions of jobs will be lost to technological advances, while millions of new jobs won't be filled because there won't be enough workers with the right skills.

We might be living in a complex and fast-changing world. However, this doesn't mean we are powerless. We have the ability to imagine future scenarios and shape our behaviour through our decisions, choices and actions that get us closer and closer to our preferred future and prevent possible unwanted future scenarios from ever happening.

In this second book, I want to continue to share with you the way to create a GREAT future that best suits and assures your health and wellbeing so you can flourish and thrive in this fast-changing world. To share with you what has helped me and others, and will help you to futurize yourself and reap the benefits of a futures mindset. A mindset that will not only change the way you see, experience and influence the world, but will also help you to anticipate and prepare for the future and act with foresight. A futures mindset that is going to have a bigger and more positive impact upon y'our future and the future of y'our future, the way you feel and lead your life, than any other development.

A good life is a life that is self-satisfying and self-fulfilling. A GREAT life is a life where you transcend yourself and are the best version of yourself in a way that best suits and assures the greater good. It is built on purpose and starts with a single question: "What the future do you want?" Keep this question at the back of your mind while reading this book. The question is the start of a (r)evolutionary process that you'll go through and fine-tune through the rest of this book and beyond.

Your choices today determine y'our tomorrow

And while imagining a better future, let's also imagine a better self. Unless we give our power away, we are in charge of creating our future.

Vlad Zachary

Before you move forward, take a step back. I want you to think about the present you. I want you to think about what you base your decisions, choices and actions on today. In other words: Why do you do the things you do? What motivates you?

I know it's not a straightforward question and there are many options. Let me give you a personal example.

My family told me that, from when I could speak, I wanted to be a cook. So when the time came, I went to catering school. When I finished catering school, I tried marketing – but failed. I stopped my studies and went to work in a hotel, then another hotel, a cruise ship… and I never imagined that I was going to do anything else in the future. Actually, I never really thought about what I was going to do next. I left life very much to happenstance, just letting events unfold, and took whatever opportunity that presented itself without much thought.

This aimless stumbling through life got me all around the world and gave me some amazing experiences. That was nice, until I got stuck and had no idea what to do next. Then a friend phoned me and asked if I would like to open a gourmet deli. His dream was to expand his business, and I was an ideal candidate. I didn't hesitate. I seized the opportunity without ever taking the time to think whether this was really good for me. I didn't know what was good for me or what I wanted and needed, as I had never really thought about it. I didn't even know that you could think about these kinds of things. Anyway, my friend's dream became my dream, and that was it. It was easy peasy, as he was the one who made the decisions and choices for me.

What about you? Whose life are you fulfilling? Have you ever stood still to think about what you base your decisions, choices and actions on?

Is your behaviour based on copy-pasting your past you? Are you in control of your future, or do you leave it up to others decide for you? What drives you? Or are you being driven?

> "Life ultimately means taking the responsibility to find the right answer to its problems and to fulfil the tasks which it constantly sets for each individual" (Viktor Frankl).

Now here is another question for you. Today, when planning your future, how far do you plan ahead? One day ahead, a week, a year... 5, 10, 20 years? This book is about the long-term future – yours and mine, for that matter, so permit me to ask these self-conscious questions.

I had never really thought about the future. Up until I was 29, copy-pasting my past or leaving it up to others to decide my fate was how I stood in life. When I opened the deli, my hopes were to get everything that my friend had as quickly as possible. A big house, big car, big motorbike, the recognition he had achieved, and his standing in his community. Oh yes – I was going to have all of that. However, two months after opening my deli, I had the first signs of suicidal depression. The business didn't work – but not only that: I wasn't my friend. My friend might have been made for running a deli; I wasn't. I wasn't used to being locked within four walls day in, day out. The deli was

Chapter 1: What, The Future?!

the end of the road for me. If I had continued leaving life up to chance or others, if I hadn't futurized myself, I know for sure that I wouldn't be here writing this today. I would have kept walking in ever smaller circles downward on the path to nowhere and one day, in a moment of desperation, I would have stepped out of life as I had planned to, to be 29 forever.

The road to nowhere, the pit of doom – that was my fate and destiny. Until I changed my modus operandi.

Again, I didn't do this on my own. I was told – rather curtly – that I was entirely responsible for the misery I had got myself into. Ouch! Those were harsh words to hear. At first, I rebelled against these words with a zillion excuses explaining that it wasn't my fault. But no truer words had been spoken. Not only had I let others dictate my path, I also had let them determine my future.

Once I recognised that I was not only responsible for my story and my future, I was ready to change. I was ready to futurize myself and make the future I wanted the cornerstone of my decisions, choices and actions.

Adopting this new mindset wasn't a walk in the park. A mindset where images of a preferred future became my North Star, my guiding light that determined my future in the present instead of my past, needed work. Lots of work – but it made sense. For the first time, I knew what I wanted and went for it.

The past had come and gone. A teacher it could be, but it didn't control my future any more. I see this all through the filter of where I am today, not from where I was. I'm telling this story because maybe, just maybe, you recognise situations, recognise yourself.

Change your story to change y'our future

My interest is in the future because I am going to spend the rest of my life there.

Charles F. Kettering

"But how did you change your story and make it into an ongoing reality, Tom?" This is a question I'm often asked. As I mentioned before, it didn't happen overnight. It was a process that I went through with help. That process included revisiting my past, finding my potential and designing my life, my future, on purpose. The future I wanted and now wake up to every day.

A preferred future that, for our purposes and needs here, could be defined as "a self-chosen, directed and personally appealing long-term image of the future I wanted to evolve into."

A future I could only envisage because I had revisited my past and been shown that I didn't have to be limited by it. A future that was also based on my potential, which I had uncovered through three questions during my "futurizing" process. Questions I was given as part of my homework to futurize myself. These three questions were: Who did I look up to and why? For what advice or problems to solve did people come to me and not to my friends? What had I done so far where I thought and wished that I could do it forever? These three questions led me to uncover my potential within. Potential that I was born with but had never recognised as such.

The importance of finding your potential is that, when developed, it can become something in the future. The good thing about using your potential to create your preferred future is that it doesn't change over time, it expands. Your potential is

Chapter1: What, The Future?!

also unique to you and doesn't exist in anybody else but you, which makes you unreplaceable in this world. The world needs you.

The aforementioned steps are how I changed my story and changed my future. I might have been good for nothing according to my past, but I had potential – and thus I could be good at something seen from a unique futures perspective. The potential I had uncovered was that in me there was a therapist, a communicator, a teacher, a researcher and a traveller waiting to be developed. The day I wanted to wake up to was one where I was a therapist who had discovered his own approach, had written a book about it and spent time giving presentations and workshops around the world.

Embracing a futures mindset started with changing the narrative of my past. This was followed by uncovering my potential, based on which I could envision a preferred future, a future I wanted to wake up to. These steps are the groundwork for the process of futurizing yourself. You can find the full story and process in my book *Futurize Yourself – Design your life on purpose.*

However, there is an important nuance that I need to explain here. The preferred future (being a therapist, etc.) that I had envisioned and wanted to evolve into was not my answer to the question of what the future I wanted. What I truly wanted was to have a good future and a meaningful life. I wanted to fit in, feel content, fulfilled, healthy and live with a sense I was evolving as a person. Today, that is still what I want, and I can't imagine that that will change over time, although conditions might change. Being a therapist who had discovered his own approach, had written a book about it and spent time giving presentations and workshops around the world – that was only the means to have what I wanted and longed for. It was what I thought I needed to develop over time to help me achieve what I truly wanted. It's important that I share this nuance with you.

The future is not what it used to be. It is changing faster than ever before, and the challenges we face are mostly of our own making. We can imagine these changes, yes. We can anticipate and prepare for them. We can have a vision of different scenarios of the future, but what the future will look like in the end still remains to be seen. It will never be exactly as imagined, anticipated or envisioned; always keep that in mind. But any way the wind blows, at the core, how you want to feel will not change. This is as much true for you as it is for all of the 8 billion people walking this planet.

Thomas Lombardo, whom I've already mentioned and will refer to a few more times, writes in his book *Future Consciousness*: "We create a good future, defined as flourishing in the flow of evolution, through the heightening of future consciousness, which is achieved by developing a core set of character virtues, most notably and centrally wisdom."

It's one of these phrases that moved me when I read it. Moved me to the brink of tears, as it described so authentically my own thoughts and futurizing process. My experience has led me to believe wholeheartedly that you create a good future through heightening your future consciousness. A futures consciousness, to be more precise. A consciousness that is created around a core set of wisely chosen, unwavering principles that will help you achieve the stability through change that is needed to evolve on purpose in an environment that is evolving faster than we are.

Again, I ask you: What the future do you want? What the future I want is also what I want you to have. So, what I want us to have is a GREAT future where we flourish in the flow of evolution and thrive in this fast-changing world. But above all, what I want is that on an individual level, you and I and all beings work towards – and actually get to – feeling content, fulfilled and healthy.

Revisiting my past, finding my potential and designing my life on purpose – that is how I changed my story and changed my future. I needed to transcend many limiting beliefs, but with my uncovered potential and the future as my ally, I again had hope and a willingness to live on. From that moment on, through my decisions, choices and actions, I evolved on purpose and became the content, fulfilled and healthy global therapist, author, speaker and teacher whose words you are reading here.

The future is not what it used to be

Times and conditions change so rapidly that we must keep our aim constantly focused on the future.

Walt Disney

As I mentioned before, we are living in a fast-changing world, with significantly different challenges from two decades ago when I started to futurize myself. Today more than ever, we are urged to think about the long-term future, not only for our personal development but also for our very survival as a species. To think about it before it is too late.

We are also more interconnected than ever before. Back in 2000 when I started to imagine my future, social media platforms like LinkedIn, Facebook, Instagram and TikTok didn't exist. Going on the internet was still via a telephone line and made this very irksome "Pshhkkkkrrrkakingkakingkakingtsh chchchcch*ding*ding*ding" sound.

Today, we are not only more interconnected virtually, but globalisation has also made the world more interconnected culturally and in terms of production and trade. We are on this planet together and we depend on each other. What happens in China doesn't stay in China – and what happens in America, Africa or any other part of the world doesn't stay there either.

Each of us is simultaneously a whole in and of itself, as well as a part of a larger whole (holon). This means we are both a part and the whole. Whatever one does on an individual level affects the other and vice versa. If the COVID-19 pandemic hasn't made that clear yet, I don't know what will.

This means that, when you think about what the future you want and what you need in order to get what you want, you need to think very carefully. Every decision or choice you make and every action you take influences the outcome of not only your future, but also the future of the people around you – people you know and people you don't know. And some decisions, choices and actions can have a global impact that will be felt for generations to come.

This is but one of the naked truths of why the future is not what it used to be. Another reason is, of course, that technology has accelerated the speed with which the world we live in is changing.

"While the past and present will undoubtedly shape the future to some degree and some artifacts from the past and the present will persist into the future, what we see as reasonable today is unlikely to be seen as reasonable in the future" (Conway, 2014). Envisioning the world of tomorrow is a challenge, and we can't be sure it will look like anything we imagined.

But all that doesn't mean we should sit back and do nothing. I hope I can instil a healthy urgency in you to think about the future and inspire you to stay hopeful and positive, but above all to take action today despite the various challenges you and we all face.

I urge you to envisage what the future you want and what the future you don't want, create scenarios of the future and raise y'our future consciousness. All that to inspire yourself to change the way you think about the future and realise that, through the decisions and choices you make and the actions you take today, you can steer yourself into the direction of the future you want.

If you opt for not taking action, leaving the future up to chance, then you will have to accept the possibility that the worst-case scenario will play out. Sure, it might turn out in y'our favour. As the future doesn't exist, it might turn out that climate change suddenly disappears and technological advances are put on hold so we can catch up. You never know – but would you put your money on it?

I know that, in turbulent times, thinking about the future isn't easy. However, that doesn't mean you shouldn't or can't do it. The world is changing in front of y'our eyes, and many challenges like climate change and the robotisation and automation of the workforce are very real. When you dig a bit deeper, you will find that the COVID-19 pandemic is but a small challenge compared to what awaits us. You can still change the tide. The future doesn't exist yet, but it is being created right here, right now.

You can align yourself with the GREAT future you want and, through the decisions and choices you make and the actions you take, make the future you want an ongoing reality.

Imagine that the worst-case scenario is unfolding today. Is that the future you want? I hope not. I want you and the 8 billion souls we share this planet with to flourish in the flow of evolution and thrive in this fast-changing world, because that is what the future I want for myself.

You want that too? Great! Then that makes two of us already.

Are you asking how? How do I/you/we create the GREAT future we all want? Continue reading, and let me and the stories inspire and guide you to take the necessary steps to make a difference for yourself and others. There is no school for this, but by doing you will learn. You will be able to learn faster, because I will share with you not only my successes but also my failures, so you don't make the same mistakes.

Oh – you are worried that the decisions and choices you need to make might not pay off for many years? I beg to differ. Unlike in organisations where big investments need to be made that won't pay off immediately, when you futurize yourself there are many nearly instantaneous benefits, benefits for your health, wellbeing and so much more. That is just the beauty of it, and in this book, I will share some examples of such benefits.

The power of futures thinking

We need a different way to make plans, not on prediction but by making plans in order to make things happen that we cannot predict and to be ready to learn.

Author unknown

One of the most important benefits of futures thinking for your health and wellbeing is that integrating futures thinking into your decisions, choices and actions helps you to be more resilient.

Futures thinking is not predicting the future. Futures thinking, sometimes also called prospection or mental time travel, is the generation and evaluation of mental representations of possible futures. "Futures" in the plural, as you can imagine and explore many different scenarios of the future.

While futures thinking is just that, thinking about the future, futurization, on the other hand, is the act of incorporating futures thinking into y'our decisions, choices and actions.

So how does futures thinking help you to build resilience?

Let's use the example of a taxi driver.

Sam is 40, is married and has three young children. He has been a taxi driver for five years. Before that, Sam had been working in a factory but, due to automation, had lost his job. Sam had never really thought about his future and became a taxi driver for a popular ride-hailing service. He only started to think about his future and that of his family as more and more passengers started asking him if he was scared about losing his job now that the development of self-driving technology has become a priority for many car manufacturers. He always replied: "Taxis without a taxi driver!? Not in my lifetime!" and left it at that.

Then one day while watching TV, he saw a report about Waymo One™, the fully autonomous ride-hailing service in the East Valley of Phoenix, Arizona. He had heard of this but thought it was a joke. He had heard that some companies were testing automated trucks – that, yes but taxis, no. He had never really paid attention to what was going on around him. However, seeing the report on fully automated taxis did trigger his curiosity, and he followed this up with a quick search on the internet. He soon found out that the automation of taxis and other transport systems was far more advanced than he realised. While surfing the web, he stumbled on the website replacedbyrobot.info.

replacedbyrobot.info is a website created by Fabian Beiner, a computer science expert and web developer, in 2015 after the publication of the academic paper "The Future of Employment: How susceptible are jobs to computerisation?" (2013) by Carl Benedikt Frey and Michael Osborne of the Oxford Martin School. According to this academic publication, about 47% of all jobs will be taken by robots.

In the search box provided, he typed "taxi driver" and not even a second later he saw that the likelihood of his job being automated in the future was 100%. When the 100% was going to be reached wasn't mentioned, but with Waymo One™ already in town, Sam knew that it was just a matter of time. The future was already here. Instead of panicking, he realised that he needed to prepare himself and look out for a new job. His kids were still young and needed schooling, and some would want to go to university. If he lost his job, it would affect his family badly. That evening, when the kids were off to bed, he talked to his wife about the future, their future.

Resilience is the capacity to recover quickly from difficulties or the ability to bounce back into shape. Chronic stress, on the other hand, is when you have lost that ability to adapt or bounce back. Chronic stress, sometimes also referred to as distress, sets in when demands on you continuously outweigh your resources, and coping and adaptation processes fail to return to ease. Stress itself is a physiological reaction that goes hand in hand with the quickening of your pulse, a burst of adrenaline and cortisol, and changes in blood flow in the body and brain which, when they become chronic and are not managed over time, lead to a wide area of health consequences if left untreated. These health consequences include physical problems like neck, shoulder and back pain; cardiovascular disease; mental health problems including anxiety, depression and a sense of hopelessness, and can lead to substance abuse.

Sam hadn't lost his job yet, and although there was an initial burst of stress and anxiety, he quickly bounced back and started to think of ways to prepare himself for the day that he would be laid off – again. This time, he was going to be prepared and ready to step into something new, as he knew that he wasn't the only taxi driver who would be looking for a new job soon.

By futurizing himself, Sam proactively prepared himself in anticipation of a future scenario he wanted to avoid and that would cause him and his family a lot of stress. He was not out of a job yet, but he used his time wisely to reskill himself. By changing his perspective and adopting a futures mindset, he embraced the future and incorporated it into his decisions, choices and actions.

Sam is a fictional character that I made up based on a TV documentary I saw about the future of work. The only difference is that the taxi driver and father of three they interviewed (who had become a taxi driver after his first job had been automated) told the interviewer he was convinced that, now trucks were being automated, his job would soon follow. However, he pinned his hopes on the government to do something about it when the time came.

While my Sam futurized himself and created a plan for the future, this taxi driver didn't. Which of the two do you think will be more stressed when taxi drivers become a thing of the past? What would also be likely to happen is that my Sam, before losing his job, would probably already have seen an opportunity and changed jobs beforehand. This is the beauty of futures thinking.

Through adopting a futures mindset, you anticipate and prepare yourself for change, but you'll be adjusting or adapting even before the change occurs. You'll always be one step ahead of the future scenario playing out.

Taxi driver is but one of the many jobs that are at risk of being automated. Other jobs, like assistant paralegal, accountant, human resources administrative assistant, insurance broker, and cashier, are but a few on the chopping block to be definitely or almost certainly replaced by robots.

> According to the website www.replacedbyrobot.info, my job as an osteopath D.O. will never be replaced by robots. But my job will change over time, or at least the demands will. If I want to be of service to my patients, I need to make sure that

I follow and prepare myself to treat new ailments. With the use of new technologies like exosuits and VR glasses, new challenges to body and mind will arise, and also new disorders. But what will happen when nanobots are the norm to measure and treat patients? Osteopathy or any form of manual treatment might not be replaceable, but it might nevertheless become obsolete.

The proactive approach

Looking for a variety of futures helps you strategise and plan for your personal future, which empowers you to create your future, not be a passive participant.

Alida Draudt & Julia Rose West

Compared to being reactive, being proactive involves any self-initiated act you do in advance to prepare for a future situation. It means taking responsibility for your life and actions rather than just watching how things unfold.

"Your futures might hold something very different than your present. By only focusing on today, or worse yet using your past to model your future, you may miss the opportunities waiting for you" (Draudt & West, 2016). Living intentionally, making deliberate decisions and choices, and doing what is needed to create the future you want and that the world needs from you. It's a mindset based on unwavering principles, but it's flexible and adaptable enough to create the stability through change needed to cope, or even to avoid unwanted changes and challenges ahead. It's a means for you to navigate the future with ease and prevent future stress from becoming a nuisance to your health, your wellbeing and your future.

You cannot solve your problems with the same thinking that created them. By taking part in y'our future proactively, you steer yourself into the future and avoid the future you don't want, avoid being surprised or, like me with my deli, ending up in dire straits.

Futurizing yourself does not happen in a singular moment in time. It's an ongoing process that often starts with making a deliberate choice or deciding to follow up on advice. A choice or decision that leads to a series of events, circumstances, encounters and questions.

When I was told I had a choice to choose my future and acted upon it, that was the start of a new trajectory and led me to get out of the big trap I had let myself be caught in. To follow up or not to follow up, the choice was mine to make and the steps were mine to take. It's a choice we all have to make and take some time in some way.

It turned out to be the best decision I've ever made and the series of events, circumstances, encounters, questions that followed were all key to adapting to a new mindset and adopting a new way of living. A way of living where I was responsible for my life, my future and all my decisions, choices and actions. The first steps were awkward but then, seeing and experiencing the benefits through wonderful synchronicities, coincidences and serendipities in my life, I just kept going.

It has become second nature to me to use the future. Now and then, I still stop and think about old or new future scenarios, and adapt based on acquired information or reflections I've had. But the main outline has never changed and never will.

A futures mindset just works for me. It's a natural fit that gave me structure, hope, meaning and purpose. It also helped me to stay calm and collected when I was challenged. On other occasions, I was able to prevent unfavourable future scenarios from playing out.

What to do with the future? One thing is: don't be fearful of the future. Also, don't fear choosing a future. I often get asked how I knew the future I chose was the right one. I didn't know. However, it did feel the right one. I was already in the worst place I could be, so there was only hope of improvement. Also, not choosing is leaving your future wide open for others to choose it for you. That future will more likely be in their interests rather than yours.

Do your homework. By that I mean: don't make a choice just on a whim when it comes to your future. Inform yourself; do the necessary introspection on what you want and what you don't want. What gives you energy, what takes it away. Use the various strategies I used and that I write about throughout this book. I didn't have that luxury, but with trial and error, I found my way. I started learning and seeing the evidence of what was good for me and what was not. Anyway, remember this: "You don't have to be great to start, but you have to start to be great." Those are the famous words of author Zig Ziglar. My dear friend and mentor Bernard Moerman, who is also a career coach, shared them with me once, and I've never forgotten them since.

The Futures Effect

It's only too late if you don't start

At the end of their lives, people often regret most their failures to act, stemming from unrealistic worries about consequences.
Paul Bloom

The future is screaming for y'our attention. We need new narratives for the future. Will you write yours? Will you design the future you want to see and evolve into on purpose? Will you, like so many others around the world, adopt a futures mindset and act purposefully today to change the course of y'our future and make it one that future generations will thank you for? Or will you stay at the sidelines and turn a blind eye, "Que Sera, Sera"?

With this book, I want to inspire you to think in a constructive way about the future and y'our say in it. An effect is a change which is a result or consequence of an action or other cause. The benefits of futurizing yourself are there for all. Not only does it help you to be ready for the changes and challenges that lie ahead of you, of us all, but futurizing yourself also steers y'our life and future in the direction you want.

> Again, the nuance of **"your"** and **"our"** is very important here. I am well aware that, for example, millions of people are currently being threatened by the effects of climate change, war, political upheaval, etc. I'm also aware that my ideas of futurizing yourself will probably be met with scorn by people faced with hunger, deprivation, or those at risk of being killed for their beliefs. Believe me, I've thought about it. There is no one solution that fits all. However, if more people become aware of the impact they can have not only

> on themselves but also on others – that actions matter on a grander scale – I hope that lives can be saved and GREAT futures can be created for all.

It is forecast that the next 10 years will bring more changes than the past 100 years. Changes that will affect the way we live, but also the way we work and work itself. The World Economic Forum (WEF) warns that one in three jobs faces the risk of being automated before the end of 2030. Are you readying yourself?

I know I'm forever grateful to the person on my path who showed me there was a different way of living and encouraged me to choose my own future, instead of continuing on the path of living someone else's dream. A future that was inevitably leading me deeper into a life of misery was not what I wanted.

I'm grateful because it turns out that the lessons I learned are an invaluable skill today.

WTF?! Knowledge is power

The power of prospection is what makes us wise. Looking into the future, consciously and unconsciously, is a central function of our large brain, as psychologists and neuroscientists have discovered — rather belatedly, because for the past century most researchers have assumed that we're prisoners of the past and the present.

Martin E. P. Seligman

Confession: I must admit that, although I had been futurizing myself for over a decade when I started writing my first book *Futurize Yourself – Design your life on purpose* in 2014, I didn't know that the term "futures thinking" existed. Nor words like foresight, future pull, feedforward, backcasting – and the list of new words related to the future goes on, as you will see in this book.

But that changed when I was writing its last chapter in 2017. It was the YouTube video "Digital transformation: Are you ready for exponential change?" by futurist Gerd Leonhard that introduced me to what is referred to as futures literacy. Since then, I've started to pay attention to the topic of futures and I've seen its popularity grow every year. I know maybe I just want to see it more – or is it a bit like the Baader-Meinhof phenomenon, also known as the frequency illusion: the phenomenon which dictates that increased awareness of something creates the illusion that it is appearing more often?

Bitten by the bug of futurization, futures studies and futures literacy, I certainly am. I can't get enough of it. I even organised a TEDx on the topic in November 2020, "TEDxVilvoorde – What The Future?!" (WTF?!). Futurizing myself had helped me to get me out of my depression, and got me to design a future I wanted to evolve into and live today. From good for nothing to actually being in demand for what I do. All that and more was because I had designed the future I wanted and created it by integrating that future into my decisions, choices and actions. I wanted, and still do, – hence this book – everyone to know how images of the future can help us overcome our challenges and create not only a good future for us but also one that future generations will thank us for.

Organising a TEDx was a good follow-up to my book to raise awareness about the benefits of "futures thinking" and adopting a "futures-oriented mindset" – the unique human features that had helped me so much. So I invited experts who, just like me, had the same passion and desire to share their futures story.

Little did I and all involved know, when we started planning the TEDx in 2019, that a worldwide pandemic would break out. "WTF?!" indeed. The TEDx was postponed, but I didn't panic and quickly decided to adapt it to an online event that would take place six months later.

What I learned from this is that what the future will bring remains a big open question, and because we never know what the future will bring, we need to maintain stability through change and be flexible and adaptable enough to navigate the changes ahead with ease.

Dealing with change also means dealing with stress, as with change comes stress. Stress is an autonomic survival response. Stress becomes chronic or turns into distress when demands outweigh y'our resources and y'our coping and adaptation processes fail to return to ease. This negative state, when left unmanaged, can lead to the weakening of the immune system, and musculoskeletal, cardiovascular and/or respiratory disease. Distress can also give rise to anxiety and depression, mood changes, memory problems and changes in time perception.

"Time perception? What do you mean, Tom?" Well, just imagine this scenario. You're halfway across a road and you see a car speeding towards you, and at that moment you start thinking about your next meeting. It's like thinking about your next meal while you are being chased by a sabre-toothed tiger. That instinctively sounds absurd, doesn't it? But have you ever wondered what it is that stops us reacting inappropriately like that?

Over thousands of years, the stress response, also called the "fight-or-flight response", has helped us to survive acute physical threats. Helped us to confront a danger or run and flee from it in a fraction of a second, and prevented you from thinking about your next meeting or meal when your immediate survival was at stake. The stress response is an excellent automated response that is still very much needed today when you find yourself in the path of an oncoming car. However, it is not a good response when it comes to psychosocial risks or threats to our existence that are a long time in the making, like climate change.

In an article entitled "Humans Wired to Respond to Short-Term Problems", Harvard psychology professor Daniel Gilbert (2006) says that: "We created an entirely new environment to which our brain is not perfectly adapted" and "the human brain evolved to respond to immediate threats but may completely miss more gradual warning signs."

So, our environment is evolving faster than we are, and the threats to our existence have changed not only in type but also in time. "Fighting or fleeing" – or "freezing", for that matter – is not a response that helps us to deal with this new environment we have created; on the contrary. Biological evolution is slow to adapt, so slow that y'our stress response itself has become a stressor.

But there is something we can do. We can futurize ourselves and evolve on purpose. I know you knew I was going to say that! What else? To deal with change is to anticipate and prepare for change. Futurizing yourself is a mindset where you embrace futures thinking and use it as a problem-solving technique to prepare for any change. I would even go one step further and say that futurizing yourself is "the" stress management approach for a GREAT future.

As I mentioned before, it becomes a way of life, anticipating possible changes and preparing for them. It's a natural process that becomes second nature, because it helps us to evolve and feel good. Nothing exists without its opposite. We need our fight-or-flight response as much as our relaxation response. While the flight-or-flight response is automatic and reactive, the relaxation response to return to ease must be undertaken voluntarily, on purpose. Thinking of y'our long-term future survival doesn't come automatically – it's something we/you need to do proactively.

No, I know we can't prepare for every eventuality, but the more you practise your future consciousness and futures skills (or as one of the speakers at TEDxVilvoorde, Walter Vandervelde, calls them: W.I.N.G. Skills – those growth skills that are less sensitive to the changing world), the more resilient you will be towards change, and the better able you will be to navigate the changes ahead with ease – and even steer the future in the direction you want and avoid unwanted futures. Futures skills – including futures literacy, futures thinking, foresight, anticipation and futurizing yourself – all stick with you for the rest of your life. That is the beauty of it.

The future is here – get used to it

You cannot escape the responsibility of tomorrow by evading it today.

Abraham Lincoln

I don't know about you, but for me, COVID-19 has been a tremendous shock to the system. Although I was personally and professionally able to adapt, this pandemic did leave its impression on me and my family. Like so many other people, I too lost several people in my close environment to COVID-19. As a wellbeing futurist, I do wonder: could we have prevented some of these deaths?

There is no denying it – yes, we could have. The pandemic itself couldn't be prevented, but we could have been more prepared for it. Especially as it didn't come unexpectedly. Experts warned of a coming pandemic decades ago (Marantz Henig, 2020). And Bill Gates voiced what scientists were saying in a TED talk in 2015. A talk that I did watch at the time but ignorantly didn't heed.

Let's not make the same mistake again. Let's raise our future consciousness and learn from what this pandemic has made visible: that the future is here and that we had better prepare for it. This pandemic has also made it very clear how interconnected we are, and how our behaviour affects other people – even people we will never meet or people on the other side of the globe.

This pandemic is a lesson that we should talk more about the future and that there is an urgent need for proactive measures to anticipate and prevent personal and global challenges from happening or getting out of hand. This might seem a daunting task. "The secret of your future is hidden in your (and our) daily routine" (Mike Murdock). "It is not in the stars to hold our destiny but in ourselves" (William Shakespeare), as "Destiny is no matter of chance. It is a matter of choice. It is not a thing to be waited for, it is a thing to be achieved" (William Jennings Bryan).

"The future starts today, not tomorrow" (Pope John Paul II). "You cannot escape the responsibility of tomorrow by evading it today" (Abraham Lincoln). Therefore, as long as we breathe, we must never neglect the future. Even though we have limited biological capacity for change, we must do what is within our capacity to change what we can change and to evolve on purpose.

We can't leave the future up to chance. Futurists and scientists alike warn us that the next 10 years will determine whether our future is bright and prosperous (heaven) or whether it leads to misery and perhaps even our eventual demise as a species (hell). Our decisions, choices and actions will determine the outcome.

Finding ourselves in this pandemic with the consequences it has caused to our lives and livelihoods, the economy and the environment is not something that happened by chance. It was the unintended behaviour(s) of "Patient Zero" that got us here. He, she or a group of people might not have woken up that morning saying, "Oh, let's change the world!" – but their behaviour did change the world and sped up an already fast-changing world. Are they to blame? No! As I mentioned before, scientists knew a pandemic was coming, but the world was not ready. Are scientists to blame? No! Let's not dwell on the past, but let's futurize ourselves and change forward, learn from this experience and "re-mind" ourselves of the importance of the future before it is too late. Without the future, there is no meaning and purpose to life, so we'd better hurry up before it's too late.

A GREAT future becomes a GREAT life

Don't ask: What is the purpose of my life, of living? Instead, ask yourself: What purpose do I want to give my life so it is worth living?

Tom Meyers

The future is not defined, and we will never be able to predict the finer details of the future, as there is not one absolute future, but many relative futures. Therefore, it shouldn't come as a surprise that futurists speak of futures in the plural. Its plurality makes the future difficult to predict to the letter, but that doesn't mean the future is a big unknown. We know, for example, that climate change will have an impact on rising water levels and mass migration. How much water levels will rise, well, that is another matter.

As I mentioned before, we also know with a good measure of certainty that technological disruption will influence millions of jobs over the next 5 to 10 years, necessitating mass reorientation plans and a reskilling revolution.

Much is uncertain – but what is certain is that y'our future, whatever it might be, is defined by y'our behaviour: in other words, the decisions and choices we make and the actions we take or do not take. That includes your individual behaviour and mine.

With all of these thoughts, reflections and insights about our behaviour and possible, probable and plausible futures running through my mind, I'm more adamant than ever about raising awareness of the benefits of futurizing yourself to help you steer y'our future(s) towards a preferable future.

I firmly believe that you will benefit from evolving on purpose to manage and be ready for the changes ahead. For that, you need to have a clear vision individually and collectively for y'our life and the future you want to create. With the future you want in mind, your decisions, choices and actions will be better informed, and you can make that future into an ongoing reality.

I'm very hopeful that you and we all can create a good future. We human beings are very resourceful. Through our mental time travelling capacity, we can imagine scenarios in the future. Inside us all, we have everything it takes to make well-considered dreams come true. I'm convinced because of my own experience futurizing myself.

Without my realising it at first, futurization has been an integral part of my life for more than 22 years. Everything I am and do today is thanks to futurizing myself and creating a new narrative of the future that I believe in and wanted to evolve into.

"Never let a good crisis go to waste," said Winston Churchill, who went on to become one of the founders of the United Nations after WWII. My life crisis was a sign that I needed to change. Since then, I've learned that change comes from within and that no one can change me but me. I've also learned that the future is a result of my decisions, choices and actions, and that my behaviour benefits my health, wellbeing, happiness, fulfilment and contentment if it is aligned to a GREAT future.

A GREAT future is a future that is Good, Resilient, Evolvable, Actionable and Transcendent for myself and others. It is not a single step in time; every step is important. Neither is it a walk in the park, or a holiday that is over after a few weeks. A GREAT future is an evolving, ongoing reality that fills you with hope, joy, contentment, happiness and fulfilment in good times and a guiding light during challenging times.

A GREAT future becomes a GREAT life and an ongoing reality through your decisions, choices and actions – in other words, your behaviour.

Yes, you can leave y'our future to chance ("Que Sera, Sera"). That is up to you to decide, but then you also have to accept the consequences of that choice. If you are not ready to change or don't know how to do what needs to be done to change, continue reading. This book is for you. This book is about defining and designing a preferred scenario of the future that is better than the one we leave to chance. A scenario based on what doesn't change over time. How you want to feel, your aspirations and your potential.

You can choose to be clear about where you are going but very flexible about how you will get there. Futurizing yourself is a mindset to evolve on purpose and create the GREAT future we all want. This isn't easy – nor is a life left up to chance. However, the benefits of futurizing yourself and living your life on purpose are way beyond your imagination and will stretch beyond your lifetime.

I ask again: "What the future do you want?"

I believe, if you boil it down, that, at a basic level, we all want the same thing. We all want to feel content, fulfilled and healthy and have a good life where we are resilient and evolve into the best version of ourself. We want to act with meaning and purpose, and we want to avoid pain. We want to leave this life knowing that we left it a better place for us being in it. We want to be good ancestors. In other words, we want to have a GREAT life – a GREAT future.

So, how do you create a GREAT future?

In his book *Future Consciousness*, Thomas Lombardo writes: "The most distinctive and empowering capacity of the human mind is to be able to consciously imagine, think about, and intentionally pursue preferable futures. We can amplify nature's vast and pervasive evolutionary process, and by doing so, we can flourish in the flow of evolution and create a good future for ourselves, human society, and the planet."

What a great summary of what I want to draw your attention to and empower you in. Yes, we use different words, but with "design your life on purpose" and "evolving on purpose", I do mean "consciously imagine, think about, and intentionally pursue preferable futures."

By empowering you to futurize yourself, I want you to flourish in the flow of evolution and thrive in this fast-changing world, and create a GREAT future for yourself, humankind, and the planet. A GREAT future that best suits and assures y'our health and wellbeing, and so much more. It assures human evolution, peace, climate thriving, sustainable economic growth, tolerance, …

A GREAT future starts with thinking about y'our past, y'our present and the future to make more informed decisions and choices that will guide your actions in the present. You need to know where you want to go, and giving it a timeframe helps you to evaluate your progress. Knowing what the future you want and need leads to informed choices, and makes it easier to make difficult decisions and take the actions you know are needed for the changes you want.

But again, when thinking about your future, some of the benefits will only become apparent when you look at the bigger picture.

You are not alone, and a GREAT future can't be achieved alone;

nor can it be achieved when we have depleted the Earth's resources or haven't limited the effects of climate change.

I know it is a big picture and thinking about it might be daunting, but it doesn't have to be. Everybody can learn and adopt a futures mindset. You are already embracing its fundamentals when you plan a holiday, buy a new car, build a house, learn a skill, …

Not choosing a future is leaving it up to chance, and what you fear might end up as a reality. Not because it was fated, but through y'our inaction. I know these are strong words and I'm sorry to use them. But it's a fact: "Only by thinking about where we want to be tomorrow can we prompt the action we need today" (WEF, 2019).

Chapter 2:
A Good Future

Flourishing in the flow of evolution is the good future, and wisdom is the means to create it.

Thomas Lombardo

The Futures Effect

What does a good future feel like?

The "good future" is a future that best supports ongoing well-being, both for ourselves and others.

Thomas Lombardo

November 1999: The gourmet deli that I had opened two months earlier was failing, and I along with it. The good life I'd imagined having my own business would bring me, including the big house, big car and big motorbike, the recognition and standing in the community, just like my friend had with his deli, quickly became a shattered dream.

How had it come to this? How was it possible that my golden ticket to success, a gift handed to me on a silver platter, turned out to be a losing streak, a financial disaster, and a personal prison from which I could see no escape?

Looking back on what seemed like a rollercoaster of short-lived ups and ever more lengthy and deeper downs, this was not what I had expected life to be. Life had to make sense and evoke a feeling of progress. Or was it all hogwash that we were meant to evolve, get wiser and become more complete in the process? I had hoped things might get better, but personally, I couldn't see it. At 29, I was a failure, a good-for-nothing. What had I learned? Nothing. And life had become more difficult year after year, not better. Progress, what progress? If anything, I was regressing rather than evolving. How did I get here? How did I get myself into this conflicted life experience even when the opportunity of the deli had seemed so promising? Surely this couldn't be what my life was all about. This was pointless, and for life to continue to exist, there must be a purpose to it. If there wasn't, why continue living?

Why continue living when life had no purpose and was only going to bring misery and pain? That was the question I ended up asking myself. I had no answer. All I wanted was to feel content, fulfilled and healthy. Content as in feeling whole, complete, no matter the circumstances. Fulfilled as in feeling in my element and doing what feels meaningful and brings joy.

I wanted to succeed in life and belong to something bigger than myself. To have a good life, like everybody else seemed to have except me. It seemed so little to ask.

I don't know your current situation, but I wonder: what does a good life – a good future – mean for you? I know it is not an easy question. But if you untangle all the complexities of life and living, if you take away all the stimuli and go deep within, what is left that is truly important? What do you want that can only be fulfilled from within?

For me, ultimately what I want today and what represents a good life and future is a feeling – a feeling of wellbeing that results in the experience of happiness. Wellbeing as a state of harmony within that is dynamic and vibrant and where I feel content, fulfilled, healthy, and in my element, regardless of what is happening externally.

Looking back, what I want today is what I've always longed and aspired to have, and I can't imagine that this feeling of wellbeing will change in the future.

It was only recently that I came to this realisation. So much had changed and was continuously changing, but how I wanted to feel hadn't changed, and I couldn't and still can't imagine that it ever would. In other words, I had discovered a constant. How interesting was that! You might now think that I've gone off my rocker, but stay with me a bit longer.

We often hear or read the quote from Heraclitus (535–475 BC): "The only constant in life is change." Turns out, as with so many sayings that we take for granted, that when you dig a bit deeper, it ain't that black and white. Like, change is not the only constant at all. The Earth orbits the Sun, and the Sun comes up in the morning and goes down at night. Gravity is also considered to be a constant – a constant that is always fluctuating around an average value. Anyway, as I said, it ain't all that black and white, and we seem to forget that – or, more likely, never really think about it. So, when I found that certain feelings I longed for were a constant in my life, like feeling content, fulfilled and healthy, that was a revelation. I knew I would not always experience those things, but I would always be striving for them. And that they were always in some way interdependent, of that I had no doubt.

The means of getting these feelings would change over time, too. What I as a 10-year-old needed to feel content, fulfilled and healthy was very different compared with when I was 21 or now at 50+ and they would certainly change later in life. But the feelings themselves are eternal.

Was I the only one who wanted to feel this way? Or, as I could imagine, is this something we all share? Intrigued by this discovery, I started to ask my patients how and what they wanted to feel, by way of comparison. To my surprise, most people I asked had never thought about it. It was so strange to see how this question seemed to make many people disappear for a moment. Disappear within themselves, and what was left was this blank stare back, accompanied by a deep silence. I could see them struggle through the question, and after a moment that seemed like an eternity, they slowly but unsteadily came back from wherever they were in their mind and refocused their gaze. When they were back, there was still no answer.

Those who had an answer I could categorise into two groups. The bigger group responded in terms of knowing what they didn't want to feel – for example, they didn't want to feel pain. The other group mostly answered that they wanted to feel happy, but when asked what else, rarely could they come up with anything more.

Why is this important? Ask yourself: why do you do the things you do? Isn't it because you want to feel content, fulfilled and healthy?

Ultimately, that is the way I want to feel, and that is why I do the things I do. Today, being an osteopath, body-centred stress coach and author is how I bring about these feelings.

In my practice, I sometimes need to go back to these roots with my patients, as some are far estranged from their own senses.

So, if I want them to feel good again, in their element, I feel that the best start is to reconnect them with their feelings, with what they want. So when they have it (for example, after the treatment), they can actually recognise it. It is also very important – in my eyes anyway – that patients have a better framework to continue working on themselves after the treatment as part of their self-management.

It is just common sense and a simple equation: by knowing how and what you want to feel, you can at any time evaluate yourself. Evaluate and be grateful for feeling in your element or, when necessary, make the decisions and choices and take the actions needed to return to feeling like that. For some, making the necessary changes isn't easy. If that is you, I hope that you will seek help. Self-management doesn't mean you have to do it all by yourself. Self-management is also seeking external help from an osteopath, a psychologist, a coach or a doctor when needed.

So, yes, as a promoter of health and wellbeing, it's important to help people have a clear image of what they want to feel. So, I ask them and coach them to think more deeply and uncover what they want to feel – which, it turns out, is more or less close to feeling content, fulfilled and healthy. Guess what? Once they've thought about it, they also feel they always had wanted this and couldn't imagine not wanting to feel this way in the years ahead. No matter which part of the world my patients come from, their age or gender, it didn't make any difference. So not only was feeling content, fulfilled and healthy a constant; it was ageless and intercultural.

Let me ask you: "How do you feel right now, in this moment?" and "What do you want to feel?" Put it into words, and if you find it easier, use a scale from 0 to 10.

How do you feel about the idea that the feelings we strive for are the ones we always want – past, present and future? That said, I've just had the insight that this is as much true for some feelings we strive to avoid, like pain. I had never considered that until now.

I know that the context and/or needs that engender these feelings might change, yes. As I mentioned before, what made me feel content, fulfilled and healthy was very different when I was 10 compared to today, and it will be different again when I'm 80, I'm sure. The world will change, and I will need to adapt, but the way I want to feel won't.

A good future will always be one where I feel content, fulfilled and healthy, and because it doesn't change, I've made it one of my anchor points, my ultimate motivation and purpose in life for which I strive on purpose.

Doing some online searching on the topic of things that don't change, I was pleasantly surprised that one of the strategies of Jeff Bezos, the founder of Amazon and the private space flight company Blue Origin, is to build on what doesn't change (Aton, 2020).

At an Amazon annual shareholder meeting, Jeff Bezos was asked about how to make long-term plans, to which he answered:

> *Well, certainly, in 10 years many things will evolve; technology will change. Machine-learning technology, in particular, will evolve very significantly over the 10-year time horizon. But I would always encourage people, when they think about 10 years, to ask the question, what won't change? That's actually the more important question. You can build strategies around things that will be stable in time. In that 10-year vision, there are a bunch of things at Amazon that are not going to change.*

With that in mind: **"On what feeling do you or will you build your future?"** It's your life, after all, so make it a good one.

What do you need to have a good life?

In order to truly upgrade your life, you can't just set goals, build morning routines, and begin acting differently. You need to reshape your environment. You need an environment that matches the future you plan to create.

Benjamin P. Hardy

I can imagine that, just like me, you too want to feel content, fulfilled and healthy – but what else? What else do you need?

What else do you need in order to have a good life that, just like your base feelings, won't change?

Although we might share the same desire to have certain feelings, what each of us needs in our life in order to have these is, of course, very different. We are all unique, with different qualities, talents, values, desires; we live in different parts of the world, have different economic means, and we are not alone.

For myself, I've defined that what I also need is a good (G), resilient (R), evolvable (E), actionable (A), and transcendent (T), i.e., **a GREAT future**. There is no way that I can live a good life without it, and so it has become my second anchor point.

> "By declaring that man is responsible and must actualise the potential meaning of his life, I wish to stress that the true meaning of life is to be discovered in the world rather than within man or his own psyche, as though it were a closed system. I have termed this constitutive characteristic 'the self-transcendence of human existence.' It denotes the fact that being human always points, and is directed, to something or someone, other than oneself — be it a meaning to fulfil or

another human being to encounter. The more one forgets himself — by giving himself to a cause to serve or another person to love — the more human he is and the more he actualises himself. What is called self-actualisation is not an attainable aim at all, for the simple reason that the more one would strive for it, the more he would miss it. In other words, self-actualisation is possible only as a side-effect of self-transcendence."

– Viktor Frankl, Man's Search for Meaning

It is a construct, but a good life is made of a GREAT future, and every element in that GREAT future is interdependent. We cannot just focus on one aspect. We are of one in body, mind and spirit and at the same time we belong to a larger whole, humanity, that lives together on a planet that is part of the Milky Way...

So, as much as we are simultaneously a whole in and of itself, we as human beings are part of a larger whole, humanity, which in turn is part of... You can fill in the rest. There is a word for this: "HOLON", a term coined by Arthur Koestler in *The Ghost in the Machine* (1967).

The element "good", as much as the other four elements discussed here in this book, is simultaneously a whole in and of itself and a part of the whole. Everything matters when it comes to having a good life and a GREAT future. These are also not the only elements we should consider when thinking of our needs to have a good future. There is the whole pyramid of Maslow, your gifts, assets, passions, strengths, potential, and meaningful work to consider, too, as you will see in this book.

Take climate change, for example. There is no good future if we don't think of limiting the effects of climate change. Already many parts of the world are feeling the effects of climate change, which will only intensify and multiply. In some parts of the world, whole countries are likely to disappear. For example, if we don't act now there will be no future for paradises like the Marshall Islands and Maldives, as they will have disappeared underwater. Cities that are on the list for being swamped are Jakarta (Indonesia), parts of Houston (USA), Venice (Italy), Rotterdam (the Netherlands), and the list goes on. Here in Belgium, even if greenhouse gases are significantly reduced and global warming is limited to below 2 degrees Celsius, sea levels could rise by between 30 and 60 centimetres by 2100 (McCullough, 2019). In total, one billion people living in low-lying coastal areas will be at risk by 2050 according to WWF Belgium (WWF, 2019).

Climate change is global change that will bring about big challenges which will cause an immense amount of distress to many people. Rising water levels are not the only problem: other regions, like the Sahel part of Africa, are already experiencing the full impact of climate change, and other parts of the world will soon be too hot to live in, causing mass migration.

I'm not a climate specialist, but I don't have to be to know what this means for people living in these areas and will mean one day for me and the people around me. A good future is not a "me" story but a "we" story – we are in this together.

In Professor Mark Maslin's latest book, *How to Save Our Planet: The Facts* (2021) he writes – and he's not the only one saying this – that: "Climate change is the greatest threat we have ever faced and the future of our planet is in our hands. — We need to develop new modes of thinking for the 21st century to creatively and collectively tackle these challenges."

Health and wellbeing will always be key components for having a good future. Always – so there is another constant for you. Y'our health and wellbeing is very much dependent on others and the health and wellbeing of our planet. So make sure your decisions, choices and actions assure y'our health and wellbeing and the wellbeing of our planet on which we depend.

The latter I addressed for the first time at a talk in Barcelona. I was asked to give a presentation for Fusion for Energy (F4E), a European Union organisation that manages Europe's contribution to ITER, the biggest scientific experiment on the path to fusion energy. I was hired to give a talk on managing stress and was wondering how I could best address this for a group made up mainly of engineers when I came across the concept of Earth Overshoot Day. Earth Overshoot Day marks the date when humanity's demand for ecological resources and services in a given year exceeds what the Earth can regenerate in that year. In 2021, it fell on 29 July, compared to 1970 when it fell on 30 December. So, every year since 1970, we have used more resources than the Earth can generate in a year. Doesn't that remind you of something? Stress! Stress is felt when the demands outweigh your resources to successfully cope. Our behaviour is stressing Mother Earth.

I don't want to scare you, but I want to raise your awareness that the future isn't what it used to be. Y'our future needs you.

How you and I take care of the Earth and of ourselves in the coming years will determine y'our fate and the fate of many generations yet to be born. Again, it's y'our future, and you can make it a good one on purpose or you can leave it up to chance ("Que Sera, Sera").

What do you need to have a good future? You need others. You need to be in your element. You need to bring into the world your innate potential, your gifts and assets. You need to develop them on purpose and put them to good use. You are of one with 8 billion souls that, like a gigantic jigsaw puzzle, interlink to be complete.

I've shared mine with you. Now, what else do you need that won't change and pushes you to action to make y'our life better?

How do you create a good future?

Think globally, act locally.

Patrick Geddes

When everything around us is in chaos and the future outlook is bleak, how can you create a good future for yourself, others and the planet? What can you do in the midst of a crisis to stay positive and hopeful? It seems impossible…

These are things I've been asked about multiple times, and I got asked them again yesterday as a question after a talk I gave on the benefits of futures thinking for y'our health and wellbeing. A talk I gave at the 5th International Conference on Time Perspectives 2021.

The participant was from San Francisco, where a heatwave was leading to record temperatures, water shortages and hundreds of deaths, bringing close to home the catastrophic consequences of global warming.

What could he do while outside the heatwave was soaring? Wasn't it too late to act? I could sympathise with him, as meanwhile many villages here in Belgium and in Germany and Austria were completely underwater due to the heavy rainfall.

I'm not a climatologist, but I believe that it is never impossible or too late to do something. I know from personal experience that, when faced with a disaster or tragedy or in the midst of crisis, one feels completely powerless. You feel powerless – but that doesn't mean you are powerless! As long as you're alive, there is always something you can do, even if it is only changing the way you look at the challenges you are facing. Viktor Frankl, Holocaust survivor and founder of logotherapy, sums it up like this: "When we are no longer able to change a situation, we are challenged to change ourselves." As long as he was alive, he had power – the power within that no one could touch.

Nelson Mandela once said: "It always seems impossible until it is done." I saw Nelson Mandela when I was working as a sommelier on the cruise ship Queen Elizabeth 2, and what I remember most is his smile. A smile that came from deep within, just like his unshakeable belief in the equality of all people and his determination to overthrow the system of apartheid in South Africa.

When you look back at your own life, I'm sure that it hasn't been smooth sailing all the time, but here you are. What challenges have you faced? What waters have you sailed? How did you overcome these challenges, these troubled waters? Think back to a particularly difficult moment that you overcame, when impossible became possible. How did you do it?

One of the principles of osteopathy is that the body has an inherent capacity to maintain its own health and to heal itself. In the same way, there lies within us everything that is needed to succeed. Within us all lie all the resources we need to create the good future we want. But success, just like good health or a good future, isn't given – it is earned and created through your decisions, choices and actions.

During a crisis, the first step is to literally or figuratively take a step back. A step back to get an overview perspective. You need to distance and calm yourself to be able to think and take stock of the situation. To think carefully about the situation or event and consider your options before you can decide what you need and/or want to achieve, aspire to, or create. Only then can you make the needed decisions and choices and take the actions that matter.

Not stepping back is like clearing a flooded cellar when the water around you is still rising. Completely bonkers! Get yourself to safety first by stepping back from danger and return to ease (reaset), and then make a plan before you act.

Professor Mark Maslin, the author of How to Save Our Planet: The Facts, writes that we need to develop new modes of thinking and start with imagining our future history where the focus is on human wellbeing (globally) as the primary measure of success, not dollars. We then need to create pathways towards this shared goal and only then act to make it happen (locally).

This is, in other words, saying: before you do anything, you need to envisage what the future you want (create your future history), design your life on purpose (create pathways) and follow up on this consciously (act to make it happen). When I read that, it was so recognisable, as these were the same steps I had taken when my business and I were failing.

Stepping back, shedding a new light on my experiences and the world around me, and then imagining what I wanted to evolve into based on my potential. Then using my envisaged future to direct my decisions, choices and actions – that was how I exited from my conflicted life experience and turned what seemed impossible at the time into an ongoing reality. I know it is easy to say all of this with hindsight. Maybe it sounds as if it was all self-evident.

I know from personal experience that, in reality, it is far from self-evident when you're in the midst of a crisis. In my crisis, my world had collapsed; my dreams and hopes were shattered. I was plagued with doubts and low self-esteem, and I was suffering enormously under the burden of the past.

Even when I had created a new narrative for my past, found my potential and designed my life on purpose, it wasn't self-evident. I was plagued with so many limiting beliefs that I had lost all hope of a good future. Yes, I could imagine that, if I was living my potential, one day I would or at least could be content, fulfilled and healthy. But that was theoretical. A far-fetched dream and an imagined reality was not a reality I was sure to achieve. A failing business and feeling depressed doesn't really fill you with much joy, hope or self-confidence. So, even though on paper it all looked plausible, I rated the likelihood that I would succeed as very unlikely.

I'd also really like to say that, once you have stepped back and created a clear idea of the future you want to evolve into, the worst is behind you and what lies ahead is easy-peasy. But unfortunately, it is not.

The rest ain't easy, nor is it peasy – far from it. But life, in general, isn't easy-peasy. However, when you know what you want, when you know why you're doing it, everything you do becomes meaningful. Meaning gives motivation, and if wanting to create a good future and a GREAT life for y'ourself isn't a great motivator, then I don't know what is. What could be more important than creating a good future and a GREAT life?

But a good future and a GREAT life don't just happen. No one gets where they are by accident. I didn't end up with my failing deli by accident, and I didn't get to be a proficient osteopath by accident either. A gold medallist in any sport doesn't get there by accident. Conscious intent is needed.

"The future awaits those with the courage to create it" (Erwin McManus).

One step, two steps, three – the future is in me

Even the greatest was once a beginner. Don't be afraid to take that first step.

Muhammad Ali

The first step is always the hardest. I was at rock bottom and had a lot of limiting beliefs and baggage to shift. I must admit: my first, second and third steps I didn't do unaided. I was a shadow of myself and, without really knowing it, I needed help to shed a new perspective on my past to see it in a new light. I also needed help to uncover my potential which, when developed, could become something in the future. The doing, however, was mine and mine alone. I needed to take the steps and realise the plan.

No one can take the steps for you. Again, you can leave it up to fate and move forward without any care for where you are going or what you'll get, or you can futurize yourself and choose your destiny. Choose and take the steps needed to reach your full potential and evolve on purpose to make it an ongoing reality.

But why is potential so important to create a good future? Yes, you may ask. Potential is your innate set of skills that don't change over time – they expand when you develop them.

As I mentioned before, one way to build (design) a solid strategy for your future is to base it on what doesn't change. So, strategically building it on the basis of your potential is of great interest. Together with the two other anchor points, it becomes a solid framework or blueprint you can use and fall back on in times of need for the rest of your life.

Putting on my cap as an osteopath and body-centred stress coach, I also see another benefit for knowing, developing and living your potential. Just imagine you're doing a job that is not within your potential, or you are promoted, based on your previous successes, into a job where you are no longer competent because you do not have the necessary skills or potential for the job (Peter Principle). What do you think will happen? Stress, that is what will happen! Lots of stress – which will not only influence your job performance but also your health and wellbeing. This kind of stress diverts you away from a good future (until you realign yourself with your potential).

A good future lies within you, within the realm of your potential – and that potential is very specific. For example: teaching is part of my potential. However, while I might be very good at teaching anyone who is interested in the body-mind and educational Reaset Approach or Futurizing Yourself, don't ask me to teach mathematics!

Working within your potential doesn't mean that life is without its challenges – far from it – but it gives you a good and meaningful feeling. It also feels so much better than when you are working outside of your potential. When working not in line with your potential, it often feels like you're permanently out of sync. I can also imagine that you complain a lot and find it difficult to motivate yourself. There is also the situation where you are in a job that is below your full potential. In this case, you probably feel bored more easily.

I ask you: "How can you have a good future or be in your element when you are doing something – day in, day out – that you don't have the potential for, fundamentally don't like or don't feel stimulated by?" I've been there, done that, got the T-shirt. That is, before I futurized myself.

However, I must nuance this. When I finally closed my deli and set out to fully fulfil my future, I did for a while take on jobs that could be considered below my potential. Reskilling myself to fulfil my future did cost a lot, so I had to work and take any jobs I could get. I knew it was temporary, a means to an end. I was, for example, hired to do filing; on another occasion, I was employed to do data input. The best job I ever had while I was reskilling myself to become an osteopath was one where I was driving to the four corners of Belgium to deposit documents at various trade registries. A job that doesn't exist any more, because a few years later it was all digitised. To pay for the last years of my osteopathy training, I went to work in a spa as a part-time receptionist and massage therapist. Working as a receptionist, like the other jobs, was definitely not my thing, but it allowed me to have financial security and the space in my mind to study.

Anyway, I'm sharing with you my experiences and insights from the past 20-plus years so that you can get some ideas, learn, and build on them. I didn't have any guidelines, and I remember how I needed to find out everything the hard way. I was only given the questions to find my potential and create the future I wanted to evolve into, as explained in my first book. The rest I had to discover on my own. I know now that I made many mistakes – took bad turns I could have avoided. Mistakes I want you to benefit from.

It's only over the past few years that I have taken time to look back and discern the patterns and coping strategies I used. A process that is very much prompted by reading books on the topic of personal futures and conscious evolution. Books that in so many ways described what I had been doing, with theories or practices that I had applied without ever being told.

For example, I was smiling and felt an enormous amount of gratitude when I read that "a good future" is "flourishing in the flow of evolution, through the heightening of future consciousness, which is achieved by developing a core set of character virtues, most notably and centrally wisdom." The shorter version of the definition of a good future is this: "Flourishing in the flow of evolution is the good future, and wisdom is the means to create it."

I read this in *Future Consciousness: The Path to Purposeful Evolution*, a book by futurist Tom Lombardo Ph.D. Further in his book, which I read a few months ago, he writes: "Contrary to economic, materialistic, technological, or environmental visions of a good future, the key to the good future primarily lies within ourselves. We need to ask, as our primary focus in creating a good future, what are the capacities within us that we need to strengthen and develop."

This is what I did… and wrote about in my first book and am building on in this one. This is what I encourage you to consider and do, so that you can have the good future I want you to experience. What I believe you need for that is to define what you want and need. Define what you want to feel, aspire to have and uncover your innate capacities, or, as I call it, your potential. With these three elements, you can create a narrative for your future. A narrative that won't change but will develop and be expressed in different ways over time.

I can highly recommend *The Cosma Hypothesis: Implications of the Overview Effect* by Frank White, *It's YOUR Future… Make it a Good One!* by Verne Wheelwright, *Think Forward to Thrive* by Jennice Vilhauer, *The Future You* by Brian David Johnson and *What the Foresight* by Alida Draudt and Julia Rose West. These are all books in which I recognised my own story. They all address how to futurize yourself, but from different perspectives and with different pathways to create the good future you want.

What is important is that you create the good future first so that you have a vision to which you can align all your decisions, choices and actions. Businesses do this, athletes as well, and you can do this too to have a future that best suits and assures y'our health and wellbeing.

The Futures Effect

Let the future pull you forward

Knowing where you are going is the first step towards getting there.

Kenneth H. Blanchard

I've said this already, but it's worth repeating: the great thing about the future is that it doesn't exist – yet. That is a good thing, because it means that, unlike the past – which has come and gone and can't be changed – you can change the future. Every decision or choice you make and every action you take influences the outcome of your future. I repeat: "Every decision or choice you make and every action you take influences the outcome of your future" – and not only your future, but y'our future. If the COVID-19 pandemic hasn't made that clear yet, I don't know what will. So, yes, it's well worth mentioning this again, and several more times throughout this book, because it is one of the keys to experiencing the futures effect and creating GREAT futures.

"Every decision or choice you make and every action you take influences the outcome of y'our future." Yes, I know I've mentioned it before. But have you ever stood still and really thought about this? When I say every decision, choice and action, I do mean literally every single one. Here is another statement I'd like you to read and then think about its implications: "Every decision or choice you don't make and every action you don't take influences the outcome of y'our future." Making or not making decisions or choices, acting or not acting – this all has an influence on y'our future.

I had never consciously thought about how my decisions, choices and actions could influence others until a patient – and this was many years ago – told me how happy her husband was when he saw that she was feeling so much better. The patient had suffered not only from back pain but also mood swings, and she had had regular crying spells for no clear reason.

I could picture in my mind how – because she was feeling better – he was feeling better and how that could influence his next call to a person in South Africa with whom he did business. I was reminded of this example recently when I had a conversation with Maxine Cunningham (Canada), the CEO of Pick My Brain, the world's first knowledge marketplace. I had explained The Futures Effect to Maxine, and the next day she told me that, after our conversation, she talked with her father about my ideas. These two moments illustrate how what we say or do and the decisions or choices we make can influence others. People we know and people we don't know, people we will never meet and people who haven't even been born yet.

So you need to know that your influence matters in the process of becoming a conscious and responsible human being and in the creation of a good future for y'ourself. As Frank White writes: "A person must first become aware of something for it to consciously affect his or her life" and: "Now that we know about and understand this reality, how does our behaviour change?" Good question! How does it change, indeed?

Another, more practical question is: "How do you know what is a good decision or choice to base your actions on?" I first needed to shed a new light on my past and uncover my potential within. The new light was that although in that moment, I felt I was good for nothing, I could become good at something. That was a big step. But good at what? It was evident that, if I was born with a specific set of capacities, I could be good at something if

I developed these capacities. The capacities I had distilled were to be a therapist, communicator, teacher, researcher and traveller. I imagined what my life would look like when I had developed these and made them part of my day. I envisaged a scenario where I was a therapist who had developed his own approach, had written a book about it, and was being asked around the world to give presentations and workshops. To that future scenario, I aligned my decisions, choices and actions, and step by step I took control over my future.

"How did you know what to do, what a good decision was?" or "How did you know that the choices you made were the right ones?" These are questions I'm often asked. At first, I didn't know. I just imagined that good decisions, choices and actions were those that led to becoming the person that I aspired to be. But, as you'll experience yourself as soon as you start developing your potential and futurizing yourself, you feel aligned with the source within you when you are doing the right thing. It's the added bonus that you become very agile when change occurs – but more about that in the next chapter.

More rationally, I would say good decisions and/or choices are those that give you an increasing sense of fulfilment, strengthen and develop your potential, and make you feel you are evolving as a person.

Making mistakes is part of the journey. Not all my decisions or choices were the right ones, I must admit. Sometimes what looked and felt like a good decision didn't always end up being one, but it was always an opportunity to learn. The most important thing I learned was feedforward, a technique that I'm still using today.

Compared to feedback, which focuses on the past, on what has already occurred, feedforward is a concept where one emphasises desired and positive behaviour in the future, uses what one has learned, and sees it in the perspective of the future. Thus, it encourages you to develop forwards.

In practice, it means for me to stop when I feel resistance, when I am challenged or when I feel out of sync. To stop and take a step back to be able to see what this challenge means in the context of the future I want to evolve into.

Stepping back helps me to reaset myself (return to ease). This is needed to be able to think clearly and take an overview perspective that allows me to analyse whether the challenge I'm facing or the distress I'm feeling is because:

A) I've deviated from my future; or

B) I'm still on the path but feel challenged to grow, become stronger, overcome a limiting belief…

Feedforward is only possible when you have envisaged the future you want to evolve into. Otherwise, you can't know whether it's A or B that applies.

Option A, as I said before, is when you've deviated from your path and you start realising somebody else's dream. Just like when I opened my deli, or when you are doing things that are not part of your potential, it is but logical that things will not flow.

But you can feel challenged (option B) when perfectly on your path and in your element – it's called growing. Let's bring up our Olympic athletes again as an example. Do you think they give up at the first, second or umpteenth challenge? Do athletes defeated in a competition think they deviated from the path? No way! After the race or game, they will step back, reaset and, most likely with their coach, review what worked and didn't work. They will think of their next event and make a plan to develop and improve to get where they want to be. This might require adapting their training schedule, taking more rest, or any other decision, choice or action that will enable them to come back into their flow again.

Feedforward has been my companion to help me keep the focus on my future and adapt when needed.

How to know what to do, how to know what would be a good decision, was ultimately all about how a decision, choice or action made me feel in the present and connected me with the good future I wanted to evolve into.

Built for a purpose

You are so busy being you that you have no idea how utterly unprecedented you are.

John Green

Now here is something interesting I read while delving a bit deeper into the beginnings of human development. It's a very short extract from one of the first chapters in the book *The Ontogenetic Basis of Human Anatomy: A Biodynamic Approach to Development from Conception to Birth* by Erich Blechschmidt.

> **Functionalism: The concept of functional differentiation**
>
> This viewpoint holds that **the human body is built for a purpose** (i.e., functionally) in the sense that the events of ontogeny (development of an organism) should be comprehensible **according to the subsequent functions of the body**. As it is known, for instance, that a hen's egg invariably develops into a chicken and never into a fish, one can speak of **the ontogenetic process having a direction by which, as it were, a design is realised**.

In other words, you are built for a purpose according to your subsequent function. From the moment of your conception to the moment you die, you are a vehicle of great potential built for a purpose. However, what started as involuntary needs to be at one stage continued and completed by your own volition to become whole.

It's like the first steps are setting the stage. From day one, there is a direction; that means a future-oriented design that you evolve into, supported in utero. (By that I mean in the womb and not the album by Nirvana.) But from the moment you are out of the womb, what then?

Wouldn't it make sense that you continue to develop according to your design? At first through the support of your parents and your environment, and then by your own volition? I know, I know: you might think I've gone completely off my rocker again. That it is far-fetched that all along you were built for a purpose. That there is some grand design…

But ask yourself: why are we all so unique? Same same, but all different… Might it simply be that what was started needs to be continued by your own volition? Is it up to you to take over and expand on the original design to give your life a direction?

There seems to be an ever-present dichotomy in life, like the aspects of yin and yang. Trillions of processes in our body function automatically, but to eat and drink, to exercise to stay healthy – these are actions you need to do. Acts that need to be done by your own volition.

Is creating a good future and living a good life such an act? I believe so, if my own experience is anything to go by, and I'm not alone in thinking this.

To quote my favourite futurist Gerd Leonhard, creator of many inspiring videos on the future including his recent production The Good Future: "The future is not something that just happens to us – it is something we create every single day, by action or by inaction. Whether the future is good or bad is entirely up to us. And most importantly: As we see the future, so we act, as we act so we become!"

How do you see ("direction") the future? It's a fundamental question as it influences your decisions, choices and actions and who you'll become ("a design is realised").

Anyway, although I'm far out of my comfort zone here, I do find it interesting that I didn't develop into a chicken but into a human being. A human being with a specific set of skills. Skills I wasn't aware of at first. I also see how my life was before I became aware of my skill set and afterwards. Before awareness, life was random and not good, and the same problems always came back – wherever I was or whatever I did. However, as soon as I became aware that I was built for a purpose, according to a futures-oriented function, and started to become who I was born to be, my life changed for the better. Suddenly, life made sense and I found means to solve the problems that had haunted me for so long.

I remember very vividly that moment when my brain started to put all I had learned about myself into some clear order. I also remember thinking that, if I was born with a specific skill set, then that had to be for a reason. I also reasoned that life would make more sense and become more meaningful when I developed my innate skills and integrated them into my life. Just as my body was made of trillions of cells all working together, not at random but according to a design, it seemed logical to me that there could be a design at a higher level that I needed to participate in of my own free will.

The Futures Effect

When the future comes knocking at your door

When the future presents itself, will you be ready for it?

Tom Meyers

Never in my wildest dreams had I imagined becoming an osteopath. It had never been on my radar until I was nearing my 31st birthday. What was also not on my radar was to ever enrol at a university, let alone hold a master's degree ("Yeah, right!"). Studying had never been my forte. In my school reports, teachers often commented that my scores were declining and that I needed to make more effort – especially for languages, including English which I failed time and time again.

Even when I had become a certified osteopath, to continue on and get a D.O. diploma had seemed impossible. But life works in mysterious ways, and with the right kind of motivation – like fulfilling your potential – and willingness, the impossible becomes possible.

I'm in awe of how time and time again, the future presented itself to make the impossible possible. For example, when I had decided to become an osteopath, I made an appointment with an osteopath in Brussels and asked him if he could help. Two months later, he came back to me and told me that his friend and colleague was starting a school in Brussels in September, which was only a few months later. I applied and, against all odds, was accepted. Against all odds, because I later heard from the school's secretary that there had been a big debate about it as I didn't really have the right background. Six years later, I was the only student who finished the course and obtained certification.

However, although the certification authorised me to practise in

Belgium, it didn't allow me to register to enable patients to get reimbursed by their social security or through complementary insurance. Talking about this to colleagues over a pint at the bar in Berlin where we were attending the yearly osteopathy conference, I was asked why I didn't enrol in the bachelor and master programme in the science of osteopathy organised by the Osteopathie Schule Deutschland based in Hamburg. That was how the future once again presented itself.

While writing this, my mind wanders off, thinking of the current situation where, for over a year now, due to the COVID-19 imposed restrictions, no physical events are allowed… No more dinners with colleagues… no more pub talks chit-chatting about life's ups and downs, the what-do-you-think-abouts… I wonder: what impact is that having on ideas, inspiration, opportunities… human flourishing? Where would I be if I hadn't had that revelatory conversation?

We all have dreams, and some find it easier than others to pursue them. If you (like I was) are laden with self-doubt and a very strong inner voice that says, "In another lifetime, I can't ever be …, I'm not good enough for …", I challenge you to futurize yourself.

My futurizing dreams came through in unexpected ways. But, just as the Buddhist proverb says: "When the student is ready, the teacher will appear", so it is too for the future: "The future presents itself when the futurizer is ready."

There are other ways the future knocks on your door that you will discover. For example, when you start the process of futurizing yourself and uncover your potential, you probably will not uncover all your potential or develop it at once.

Uncovering your potential is in many ways like learning a skill.

When you learn a skill, you start with the basics. Then, with practice and time, you get better – but you also discover that some skills lead to other skills which you integrate or build on. For example, my dad, who has become a skilled sculptor (www.sculpturesmeyers.com) started with painting, then discovered during one of his many art classes that he had a knack with metal. I remember his first origami-like sculptures made from food cans. We had cats in the house, and as soon as a can was empty, he was practising his cutting and folding skills on them at the kitchen table. After a while, he moved from the kitchen table to the shed in the garden, where he could use a soldering bolt to make bigger pieces. Now he lives in France, where he has even more space and creates monumental sculptures in corten steel and inox. Today, you can find his sculptures on market squares like in Changy (France), and towns including Autun (France) and Château Chinon (France), as well as in private collections around Europe and beyond. My dad was born an artist in an artistic family. It was my grandad who taught him how to paint and make figurines in wood. He stopped painting when he got married, I was born and his time was consumed between family, building a house and working as a computer programmer.

He picked up painting again some time after – due to restructuring – he was laid off from work. He was 47 when he lost his job, and a career coach told him that, if he had a dream, it was now that he could make that dream come true. That is when the artist in him reawakened, and he dedicated himself fully to developing his skills. It was during one of his art courses that he started to work with metal and felt that with metal he had something special. Something others also felt; they pointed out to him how unique his technique and work was and encouraged him to pursue this path further. He took that feedforward to heart and became very successful at it.

When Dad told me this story some years ago, I immediately recognised how similar his journey was to my own. In my book *Futurize Yourself – Design your life on purpose*, I mention how Agnes, with whom I took the first lessons in the art of manual healing, saw my potential and on the second evening of the course, asked if I had done this before – I hadn't. She had seen the ease with which I performed the different gestures, that she hadn't seen in others and encouraged me, gave me inspiration, and helped me to pursue my new-found vocation. That I specialised in body-centred stress coaching was also prompted in a similar way. As soon as I opened my osteopath practice, patients reported that after their consultation they not only had improvement in their physical condition, but they also noticed improved cognitive abilities, better concentration and experienced less stress. I was often asked what I had done, because it was something they hadn't experienced with other osteopaths. At first, I just put it down to osteopathy being a holistic treatment approach and didn't really pay much attention to it. When more and more patients, young and old, from different backgrounds, came back with the same experience, I became intrigued, and it was then that the researcher in me awoke. That awakening led to the development of my own approach. A novel body-mind and educational method of healing that I call the "Reaset Approach" – which, in turn, awoke the teacher and communicator in me.

So, just like my dad, I didn't come into all my potential at once. It was a gradual process. However, unlike my dad, when I experienced my life-changing event I didn't have a dream I wanted to fulfil, nor did I know what potential was in me. I created a dream based on the potential I had uncovered. Envisaging my dream or, as I like to refer to it, the future I wanted to evolve into, helped me, when an opportunity presented itself, to grasp and develop it. That is how I seized the moment to develop the therapist in me; seven years later, it was time for the researcher to emerge and two years after that the communicator and teacher, and so on. It took me nearly 10 years to grow and evolve into my fundamental skill set. Only after all that did I discover there was still more potential to uncover.

As I mentioned before, you will discover that your potential is not limited to what you first uncover. Some aspects only emerge later, when you are ready. For example, it was only a year ago that I discovered there was a facilitator – people manager – in me, someone who helps a group of people to work together towards a common objective, and plans how to achieve this objective, during meetings or discussions.

Something I thought I didn't have in me. This was reinforced by the fact that, on all the occasions I had been professionally in a supervising or management position before, I had failed at it. Not only was I not good at it from a management point of view as I lacked the needed (overview) vision, I also couldn't handle the physical and mental stress that came along with it. As far as I was concerned, I could manage myself and that was it.

But then a couple of years ago, after attending a barbecue of the Belgian chapter of the Professional Speakers Association (PSA), I received feedback that made me question my self-limiting belief.

It turned out that the barbecue took place in a very busy tavern with no separate area for the guest speaker, Bernard, to give his talk. Bernard rightfully refused to speak under these conditions. As I was familiar with the organisation and knew the organiser, and because I just like to know what is going on, I was involved in the discussions to find a solution.

Long story short: over the next two days after the barbecue, I had two members phone me. One was Bernard, whose talk had been postponed to another occasion. I had only met and spoken to him once, very briefly, a year earlier. After the initial chit-chat, he said: "Tom, I have to tell you something. I don't know why, but at the barbecue, I thought you were the chairman of the organisation."

A bit dumbfounded by this comment, I asked him: "What do you mean?"

"Well, Tom, I can't really explain, but there was something about your presence, your calm and the way you stood and spoke to help resolve the situation that, at one stage, I really thought you were in charge. But I knew you weren't. It was a very strange experience, and I just wanted to share that with you," he said. The second member that phoned me in the days following the barbecue ended up saying nearly the same thing.

I truly believed that there wasn't an ounce of leadership potential in me. But being praised twice in a couple of days – that intrigued me and, instead of downplaying what they said, I thanked them both.

PS: If someone pays you an honest compliment, accept it and thank them. Don't say "It was nothing," because that is telling someone who has had the courage to say something nice that you don't value their judgement. You might not believe what they say in the moment – but still acknowledge their courage by saying, for example, "Thank you! I appreciate you saying that."

Their kind words kept on turning in my mind over the next few days. What was happening here? I rarely get praise, and here I was being praised for something – not once but twice – when I wasn't aware that I had done anything noteworthy. It tickled my curiosity. Now that I'm writing this, I'm wondering if curiosity could be considered as a form of potential, a personal trait. Or is it part of my potential as a researcher? I can't imagine a researcher not being curious.

Anyway, what was happening? Let's come back to the second question that helped me uncover my potential. Question 2 in the Futurize Yourself process of finding your potential is: "For what advice or problems to solve do people come to me and not my friends?" Through this question, I had found out there was a therapist in me. Now, what was this experience telling me, if it was telling me anything? That there was a leader in me?

Over the next few days, I just couldn't let it go. I replayed the event as a film in my mind, or at least what I remembered of it, and started to let my mind wander to other recent experiences and memories.

Thus, my mind wandered to the time I organised meetings in Brussels for the same speakers' association, the recent yearly holidays with friends to Slovenia and Croatia that I organised from A to Z… and then it hit me. Like a flashbulb going off in my head, I suddenly realised that I had been organising and facilitating people to come and/or work together towards a common objective. For example, the events in Brussels: no one had told me to do that. I had come up with the idea, got the board of the association to agree to it, organised the location, the speakers and the invitations, and recruited a small team to make it all happen.

Chapter 2: A Good Future

That's how in this case I started to realise that my limiting belief no longer had any basis. I had been organising regular events and our yearly holidays with friends…! Plus, I was seen as a people manager by others. Who was I kidding but myself?

The conversation I had with myself was something like this: "Tom, the two times you did fail as a people manager were, what, more than 20 years ago? Don't you think you might have evolved since then and that what you think is a limiting belief?"

"It looks like that, but how would I know? This might all be circumstantial."

"Well, organise another and bigger event and see how you feel in the process."

That is what I did. I contacted a few speakers I knew and asked them if they would be interested in organising an event on the benefits of futures thinking. That idea eventually turned into a TEDx, TEDxVilvoorde, with the theme: "What The Future?!" What else! From an organisational point of view, it was a success, even though, due to the COVID-19 lockdown measures, I had to postpone the TEDx and change it from a live on-stage event to a digital event. Not only was it a success; with it, my limiting belief became history, and managing people towards a common objective – a good future – is now a quality I'd like to develop further. PS: If you want to see that TEDx, go to my website www.futurizeyourself.com – there is a link.

It's through moments like these that the future comes knocking on your door. Often unexpectedly – but when you work with your future, you know when to stop and step back to witness, learn, and evolve into your full potential.

The future of possibilities

When you think you are no longer able to change a situation, you are challenged to think how you feel about the situation and change yourself.

Tom Meyers

As you can witness from what I have shared so far, although I had a clear view of the future I wanted to evolve into, it was not a fixed future. On the contrary, it was open-ended and symbolic. For example, when I envisaged being a therapist who had developed his own approach, it didn't specify what kind of therapist or the approach. When you're thinking of designing the future you want to evolve into, please keep this in mind.

You can be more specific, I have no doubt about that. How you design your future depends on a variety of factors like age, experience and whether you have to start from zero or are already a hero. Yes, even if you are already a hero, you can benefit from futurizing yourself to evolve further and/or stay on top of your game.

To be clear: futurizing yourself is not about being precise or predicting your future. It's about looking at possibilities, probabilities, and endless opportunities.

Futurizing yourself is a mindset where you are developing the tools to give direction to your future and shape it in a meaningful way. This mindset helps you to be more prepared and resilient to navigate the changes ahead with more ease and gives you the means to deal with unexpected changes.

The future is always in the making and, yes, there are drivers that shape the future which are outside your control. Futurizing yourself is a form of self-care. By narrowing your perspective to yourself – to what you can do to shape your future in the context of what is going on around you or what might happen – you will be more prepared and resilient, and you will have less stress, when something unexpected happens.

This has always been a useful skill, but it is essential today in order to navigate the fast-changing and challenging world we live in. A good future doesn't just happen; it is created from within. Created through your decisions, choices and actions. How often have you stood still and thought about the fact that you shape your future? How often have you stopped and thought about the consequences of your decisions, choices and actions or inactions? How often have you thought about what a good future means for you and about shaping it on purpose?

Don't wait until it's too late and you find yourself left regretting the steps and opportunities you didn't take to shape y'our life into something GREAT.

Questioning the meaning of life, our purpose or what is important often arises when it is too late, or in our deepest and darkest moments. Isn't it fascinating that in times of transition or crisis, we see the light? My own life crisis was the starting point of questioning the meaning of life, giving my life a purpose and evolving into it. I also often see in patients how a life crisis has made them think of the more important things in life, their spiritual needs.

Spiritual needs as in the needs and expectations with which humans find meaning, purpose, and value in their life. Such needs can be religious in nature, but even people who have no religious faith or are not members of an organised religion have belief systems that can give their lives meaning and purpose

(Murray et al. 2004).

One of my patients, a 49-year-old man who had been in a COVID coma for two and a half months, told me that his big lesson from this life-threatening experience was that he had never taken care of himself. Something I had to remind him about a couple of months after the first session. I hadn't seen him for a month, and I was shocked to see that he had gained a lot of weight. I pointed this out straight away – in a diplomatic way, of course, as I didn't know how he would take it. He told me he had started working full-time again but had less to do, and when he got bored, he ate. Ate high-calorie chocolate bars. He also confessed later that, in the same period, he had not been so diligent about doing the exercises that were needed to help him recover from bilateral foot drop (a general term for difficulty lifting the front part of the foot), the condition he had consulted me about and which physiotherapy hadn't been able to resolve.

So here was a man who was lucky to be alive, whom I'd helped to regain control over his feet so he could walk normally again. A man who had been working hard for months to recover – and, now that he was nearly fully recovered, fell back into his old pattern! Holding the proverbial mirror in front of him hit home. The difference at the next appointment two weeks later made me very happy. He radiated energy that I had missed seeing during his last visit, and he had lost weight. He also walked with more confidence and without the need of his foot braces. He was back on track, yes! Every time I've seen him since, he tells me how the mirror helped him and continues to help him evolve.

I share this more recent example of a deep insight after trauma with his permission. It typifies what I hear so often from patients and know from my own experience: how life crises make us think about the more important things in life. However, the question I've asked myself on several occasion over the years is: Do you (I/we) need to go so deep down the rabbit hole to change our behaviour and attitude towards a more meaningful future or to start fulfilling our purpose in life?

Take an overview perspective

Life is about perspective and how you look at something... ultimately, you have to zoom out.

Whitney Wolfe Herd

In psychology, there is a term for positive psychological change experienced as a result of adversity and other challenges, and that is "post-traumatic growth."

It is, of course, a good thing that illness or adversity can change our relationship with ourself, our environment, give us a deeper sense and meaning, and alter our attitude towards the future. Not all illnesses or traumatic experiences will do that, though, and again I wonder if we really need a traumatic experience to alter our life and change our behaviour for the better.

I don't think we do, but too often it is the way. However, there are many ways to tune in to life lessons without needing to go down the rabbit hole – for example, if today you start to futurize yourself and act upon that feeling or dream you've been neglecting. If you are unhappy today, you can get help and find out why you are unhappy, and through your decisions, choices and actions, you can do something about it going forward. You can shape your future, or you can leave it to others to shape it for you and forfeit your happiness. Recently I heard management consultant and co-author of the book *The Power of Pull*, John Hagel, say in a podcast: "Small moves, smartly made can set big things into motion." This very much accompanies the Zig Ziglar quote I mentioned earlier: "You don't have to be great to start, but you have to start to be great."

A life-changing experience for a GREAT future starts with small

Chapter 2: A Good Future

moves, smartly made. In the end, it is up to you. This book teaches you how to drive safely and navigate the changes ahead, but you must become the actor and driver that shapes your future on purpose. It is your life, after all. It is yours to shape and create.

What the future do you want?

Yes, here is that all-important question again. As we've been zooming in on various aspects of futurizing yourself, it is good to take a moment to zoom out again. So stop reading, breathe slowly in and out, and zoom out to see your full picture. See your past and the future you want to evolve into, and observe your present. In your mind's eye, see the journey. You are a work in progress, simultaneously a whole in and of itself as well as a part of a larger whole from a cosmic perspective. In this moment you are focusing on the part: focus on what a good future entails for you and what you need in order to evolve into that good future which, in itself, is part of a GREAT future for you and humankind.

Observe your feelings. Write them down.

It is essential to stop now and then. The good future is in the making, but it is also here already. When you are futurizing yourself on purpose, the future is part of your present. When you brush your teeth, you do it to have strong teeth and prevent gum disease or cavities in the future, and at the same time, you benefit from an attractive smile as you remove any traces of your last dinner from between your teeth and are left with fresh breath in the present.

Futurizing yourself – the conscious act of designing a GREAT future and incorporating it into your decisions, choices and actions – is just like brushing your teeth: preparing for a good future but also with benefits in the present. You are a work in progress, and life is a journey – not a destination. So make sure you raise your awareness in the moment, and enjoy the moment and the journey.

You are amazing, so be good to you, be good to y'our future, always.

Chapter 3: A Resilient Future

At the heart of resilience is your ability to adapt. This refers to making adjustments – physical, emotional and mental – based on new circumstances and information. Adjustments can be in your behaviour, perception, beliefs or judgements. The more effective you are in adjusting and changing, the healthier and more resilient you will be.

Stephen Sideroff, Ph.D.

Best wishes for your future

I am tomorrow, or some future day, what I establish today. I am today what I established yesterday or some previous day.

James Joyce

I wish you to have a good life and pursue a GREAT future. A life where you can realise your inner potential and turn it into an ongoing reality. I wish you and everyone on Spaceship Earth to flourish in the flow of evolution and thrive in this fast-changing and ever more challenging, complex but also intriguing world full of opportunities. Yes, also opportunities – that is, when you know how and where to look for them. I also wish that you will go forward with hope and determination, and in the best possible shape in body, mind and spirit in an environment that flourishes and thrives with you. To achieve all of that and more, you will need resilience.

> **Resilience** (Oxford Dictionary):
> - The capacity to recover quickly from difficulties; toughness
> - The ability of a substance or object to spring back into shape

My definition of resilience is: "Y'our ability to adapt and/or bounce back from adversity and return to ease" or even more succinctly: "Y'our ability to reaset." Ease being that dynamic state between stress and relaxation, a state from which you can quickly and successfully adapt or adjust to new circumstances, challenges or demands. Other people, like Barabasi, the author of *Linked: How Everything Is Connected to Everything Else and What It Means for Business, Science, and Everyday Life*, define resilience as a system's ability to adjust its activity to retain basic functionality when errors, failures and environmental changes occur. Whatever definition you use, being resilient doesn't mean you won't experience stress, challenges or changes. Life always has its ups and downs, pushes and pulls. Resilience is constituted of the resources you have to be able to adapt and come through these changes and challenges without harm and, in best-case scenarios, stronger.

In a fast-changing world, your ability to adapt and maintain stability through change will be challenged and tested on many levels. How well you will adapt, navigate or adjust to the changing environment will define your future, your health and wellbeing, your career, your relationships and just about every other aspect of your life.

So, how resilient are you? How, for example, did you cope with the many changes and challenges COVID-19 brought along? Were you able to adapt easily, stay cool and composed, or did you become anxious? How did you do job-wise? Were you able to maintain financial stability or did you find yourself with no income or a reduced income? Did you find it easy to be in lockdown or to work from home?

For you who are reading this book a hundred years from now and haven't lived through this pandemic, think of some major personal or global upheaval that caused a major life change or demanded an enormous effort on your part. How well did you go through the (e)motion? Were you able to bounce back easily?

Anytime is a good time to zoom out and look back to learn from and build on your experiences, but the earlier the better.

The question you are probably asking now is how you can become more resilient in order to have a GREAT future. The first step is becoming aware of your ability to adapt and bounce back from a setback or change in your environment that the future might bring. You can do this by imagining some future scenarios and seeing how ready you are to deal with them.

For example, think of your current job, house… and how well you are prepared to adapt if you would suddenly lose it? How well will you deal with another pandemic or with a power or communications outage due to a big solar flare with coronal mass ejection (CME)? A what? Look it up and you will see that, for example, power blackouts have happened in Canada (1989) and Sweden (2003) following small solar eruptions. The last (to date at the time of writing) major X-class solar flare erupted on 3 July 2021, and smacked into our planet's atmosphere eight minutes later. Luckily for us, this solar flare happened at the edge of the Sun's face and the CME wasn't in the direction of the Earth, but it is only a matter of time. A severe solar storm that would blast the internet offline for many weeks or months happens once in a century, and it has been a century since the last one.

Furthermore, how will you deal with worsening climate conditions? As regards climate change, well, I don't think I need to tell you how real it is. The latest assessment report (2021) by the Intergovernmental Panel on Climate Change (IPCC) states that the effects will happen more quickly and get worse over the next 30 years before things get better. Whether things actually do get better will depend on what we do as individuals and collectively today.

I know that all sounds very dystopian, but forewarned is forearmed. Some events we cannot prevent, like a CME or the recent huge underwater volcano eruption devastating the island of Tonga (14 January 2022). However, we can do our best to prepare ourselves against the consequences by working out "what if", "if this then that" scenarios. Still, we must not forget, and we need to accept, that the best-laid plans don't always go as expected.

Having a futures mindset helps with all of these. In their book *What the Foresight*, Alida Draudt and Julia Rose West write: "While you may design the most amazing future visions for yourself, somewhere along the road your vision will be forced to change" – "A futures mindset allows you to articulate long-term goals and provides you with the knowhow for agile adjustment when change occurs." So true: a futures mindset is a mindset that has learned to be agile, i.e., knows how to react quickly and one that through foresight recovers quickly, i.e., is resilient.

Prepare for the future or you risk being late for the future. The future arrives more slowly than you think and faster than you can imagine. What was once thought to be science fiction has become science fact. Again, forewarned is forearmed.

Your ability to futurize yourself, which includes optimising your resilience, will be key – and will define how you deal with it and determine the long-term outcome of our future and the future of humanity.

I ask the questions again: "What the future do you want?"

Do you want to have a good life? Then create a GREAT future. Do you want to feel content, fulfilled and healthy in a fast-changing world? Do you want to be a GREAT steward of the Earth for your children, your children's children and generations to come? Yes? Then you know what you need to do – and you need to do it NOW.

The push and pull of the future

Social change will be viewed as a push-pull process in which a Society is at once pulled forward by its own magnetic images of an idealised future and pushed from behind by its realised past.

Fred Polak

Now is the time to do what was timely yesterday but essential today. Don't wait till you have more time. Don't wait till whatever you think needs to be over first is over before you start doing what you want and need to do. Do it now. Take that first step. There will always be something in the way if you don't start.

For a GREAT future, you have to aspire to be GREAT. "You can expect the future to take a definite form or you can treat it as hazily uncertain. If you treat the future as something definite, it makes sense to understand it in advance and to work to shape it. But if you expect an indefinite future ruled by randomness, you'll give up on trying to master it" (Peter Thiel).

I know I'm repeating myself here, but what the future do you want?

Life is always in motion and full of challenges. Life doesn't give us a break until we take a break. Food or drink doesn't come into your mouth unless you put it there. You can be the greatest writer of all time – but if you don't put pen to paper, no words are written, and the opportunity is lost to the moment that was never seized. Some things just need to be done. Long-term futures thinking is not something we do automatically; it has to be done on purpose, by our own volition.

We have the innate ability to time travel – and, if you really think about it, you do it constantly. For example: when planning a wedding, your next meeting, picking up the kids later from school, when grocery shopping. We are continuously planning short-term future events. However, thinking long term – for example, envisaging what you want 10 years from now or longer – most people just don't do it. It doesn't come naturally. There are several reasons for this; one is how our brain has evolved, and another is because, the further into the future we look, the less certainty there is.

However, times have changed, and the future will become a series of stressful events if we don't change our ways. To change our ways, we need a futures mindset. We need long-term meaningful objectives/goals that will help us to make better decisions in the present. "Goals are how we paint the picture of a future we're motivated to work towards" (Jory MacKay). By future goals, I don't mean the nitty-gritty stuff – that's impossible – but rather to have the bigger picture in mind at all times. This needs to become a habit.

In a recent motivational talk I gave to students of the RNB Global University in Rajasthan, India, I ended by saying: "Don't wait for it to be too late and be left with regrets for the steps you didn't take, to shape your life into something GREAT."

Life tends to steer us away from what truly matters. It's as if we are continuously being distracted from the essence of life. The question is: who or what distracts us, and why? We can say it is due to such and such, but in the end, it might be best to look in our own bosom to see who ultimately lies at the basis of this distraction.

Life is always in motion – a push and pull of various forces (stressors) with different levels of intensity and duration that steer us in a particular direction. These can be physical, psychological, social or spiritual forces, real or imagined. Imagined – really? Yes, really. How many fear or feel anxious about the future while it doesn't exist yet?

But ultimately it is within ourselves to choose how we react to the push and pull of life. A captain of a ship can leave the steering of his ship up to fate or he can steer it in the direction of a chosen destination. A captain can choose a direct line from A to B or do it in a zillion other ways. He or she might also encounter obstacles but is trained to make decisions to act in time when needed to deviate from danger while staying on course.

I remember the lure of distraction when I was studying to become an osteopath. I was working full-time to be able to pay for my classes and the apartment I was renting at the time. So time was limited, and the time I had I needed to study. Being in my early thirties and single, one part of me, rather than studying, wanted to go out and mingle. Every weekend I could have gone out with friends, but 9 times out of 10 I said no to the invitations. That was always difficult, but my goal was very clear: I wanted a better future, and that required my time. The good thing was that being focused gave me the necessary motivation to pass the various tests and papers I needed to write. So keeping my focus wasn't all bad. On the contrary, it gave me more qualitative time with my friends when I saw them. Life made more sense and became slowly but surely more fulfilling and whole. In the end, look where it got me. Of the 12 that started the osteopathy course with me in Brussels, I'm the only one who completed and passed the final exams five years later.

Again, I didn't know at the time that I was using futures thinking, anticipatory personal leadership and foresight tools to motivate and steer me into the future I wanted. I was just told that I had a choice in making the future I had chosen on purpose into an ongoing reality. Once told, I felt it was evident. "You want that future? Well, what are you waiting for?" In my echoic memory, I can still hear Eline, the psychoastro consultant who had helped me so many years ago (read the full story in my first book), saying those words after I had shared with her the answer to the question what an ideal day would look like for me 10 years in the future. Today I am living that future and sharing it with you, along with all the learnings I can think of that I've had between then and now.

Say hi to the primordial futurist

As one philosopher noted, the human brain is an 'anticipation machine' and 'making future' is the most important thing it does.

Daniel Todd Gilbert

Futures thinking, anticipation and foresight might be words that are all new to you, but these are things you've been doing all your life. Your body, through its senses, is – and has always been – scanning and anticipating its environment. Neuroscientists commonly call the brain an "anticipation machine". To predict and get ready for what is going to happen next, it constructs a perceptual filter that selects and organises what we actually become aware of based on what we've experienced before (Daniel J. Siegel).

Scanning for the next possible dangerous or stressful situations, and anticipating the processes needed for digesting your next meal.

For example: you've just taken your favourite cake out of the oven and you take in that sweet smell that makes your mouth water. Stop there: what just happened? Why does your mouth start to water?

It starts to water because your body is anticipating what it needs to prepare the mouth and the digestive system to deal with that cake. Further down the digestive tract, your stomach is also preparing itself to welcome your cake. All of that goes on when you smell or see food.

Even now, just thinking about making or eating a delicious cake with lots of chocolate, or cream, your favourite topping or filling can make your mouth water and your stomach create digestive juices and enzymes.

The truth is that from the time of conception your body is futurizing itself. "Futurizing" as in incorporating futures thinking into its decisions, choices and actions. How's that, Tom?

Well, let's go back to something I mentioned before in Chapter 2.6, "Built for a purpose": Functionalism. I hope you don't mind that I repeat the paragraph plus one more sentence, from one of the best embryology books.

Embryology is complex, so I won't bore you with it further after this, but this is interesting and worth repeating.

> **Functionalism: The concept of functional differentiation**
>
> This viewpoint holds that the human body is built for a purpose (i.e., functionally) in the sense that the events of ontogeny (the branch of biology that deals with the development of an individual organism) should be comprehensible according to the subsequent functions of the body. As it is known, for instance, that a hen's egg invariably develops into a chick and never into a fish, one can speak of the ontogenetic process as having a direction by which, as it were, a design is realised. According to this viewpoint, the process of ontogeny is similar to goal-oriented or teleological (relating to or involving the explanation of phenomena in terms of the purpose they serve rather than of the cause by which they arise) movement.
>
> (Blechschmidt, 2004)

Chapter 3: A Resilient Future

At your conception, the fusion of your mother's egg cell and your father's sperm cell didn't multiply randomly but developed on purpose. The development of the human embryo is very complex and influenced by many factors that shaped you into who you are today.

You developed into you as I did into me, through a design that was not outside of yourself (your mother's fertilised egg cell) but within yourself, but also influenced by forces outside of yourself. Developmental movement, the way we grow, is always occurring against resistances, and that influences the outcome. The outcome is also dependent on when something or some part develops. In other words, it is time dependent.

To futurize yourself by designing your life and evolving on purpose is not any different. It is – when your consciousness is ready – to evolve in the sense of your future history and progress, by your own volition, into the person you were born to be. That development is dependent on your environment, on the resistances you'll experience, but also on when you started. I was lucky to have had my existential crisis at 29, with lots of time ahead of me to develop into the person I was born to be. But imagine I didn't have that "Aha!" moment until I was 58. Not only would the condition from where I started to futurize myself be very different, but so also would be the time left for me to develop my potential. But anytime is the right time to start – but you have to start sometime.

Remember, I'm an osteopath and body-centred stress coach, and I see the world from the perspective of the body. The body that keeps fascinating and inspiring me as I work with it every day. So, if you hear me making reference to the body, you know where that comes from.

Your body as the primordial futurist – I bet you didn't see that one coming! But think about it. Every moment of the day, your body anticipates and adapts itself according to inner or outer stimuli to keep you alive, to keep you upright, to digest the food you eat or will eat and for a zillion other reasons.

For body systems like blood pH or body temperature, this adaptation – to keep the necessary steady state – is within very small operating ranges. That process is called homeostasis. Homeostasis, from the Greek words for "same" and "steady", refers to any process that living things use to actively maintain fairly stable conditions necessary for survival.

When the adaptive changes needed to maintain stability through change are broader – for example, to deal with stress, and predictable and unpredictable events – then the process is called allostasis. Allostasis proposes that efficient regulation requires _anticipating_ needs and preparing to satisfy them before they arise, as opposed to homeostasis, in which the goal is a steady state (Sterling, 2012).

The advantages of allostasis, according to Sterling (2012), are: (i) errors are reduced in magnitude and frequency; (ii) response capacities of different components are matched – to prevent bottlenecks and reduce safety factors; (iii) resources are shared between systems to minimise reserve capacities; (iv) errors are remembered and used to reduce future errors. This regulatory strategy requires a dedicated organ, the brain.

You might be rolling your eyes by now and thinking "Whatever". But hang on a bit more. This is all useful in the bigger scheme of things and my wish for you to experience all the benefits of the futures effect and to be futures ready so you can flourish and thrive in this fast-changing world.

To be futures ready and ahead of change, you need to be futures minded. That means you need to become very good at anticipating your needs and prepare for changes and challenges before they arise, as opposed to reacting to them. That is not only in body and mind but also regarding changes that might happen in your field of work, your environment and being ready for the next pandemic.

Personally, and as an osteopath and body-centred stress coach, I see first-hand how people are already suffering from life changes or the push and pull of daily life today. But if this is already such a problem, what will it be like tomorrow? A tomorrow where everything is intensified.

How can we – you and I – stay healthy in this fast-changing and challenging world? This question concerns me deeply – not only professionally but also on a deeper personal level.

Here below is an article I wrote during the COVID-19 pandemic entitled Futurize Y'our Workforce's Health and Wellbeing (3 December 2020). This article was written with business leaders and organisations in mind, but, as you will see, it is really addressed to you and expresses my deep concern going forward.

Futurizing Y'our Workforce's Health and Wellbeing

The next 10 years will bring more changes to humanity than the past 100 years. (Gerd Leonhard)

Summary

In these fast-changing times, taking care of employee health and wellbeing with clarity is vital for creating a good future where employees flourish and organisations thrive. This will require a new holistic and future-minded collaborative approach to health and wellbeing which promotes personal health responsibility and futurization. A holistic approach that incorporates futures thinking on purpose and enhances employees' ability to adapt, self-manage (health) and flourish in the flow of evolution (wellbeing).

Background

In times of change and any other time: "Mind your body before your body reminds you."

We are living in a fast-changing and challenging time. A time when entire populations are under immense pressure due to the COVID-19 pandemic, which is devastating lives and livelihoods and which has triggered a global economic crisis with far-reaching implications. But we are also living in a time where, due to new emerging technologies, job skills and working conditions are changing, and millions of jobs are at risk of being automated. Furthermore, while all this is going on, let us not forget that climate change is affecting our natural environment, fuelling conflict and mass migration in many parts of the world, and also harming our health and wellbeing, global security and world peace.

In these unsettling times, with everything changing so rapidly and so extensively, there is a great need to find stability and clarity, something to hold on to while everything changes.

This requires new ways of thinking on the part of organisations and the workforce alike. New ways of thinking not only to secure the economic aspects of the organisation but also the heart of every organisation – which is the health and wellbeing of the workforce.

Fostering a healthy and happy workforce is a vital factor to enable organisations to flourish and thrive in these fast-changing times. It is not only good for business because happy employees are more engaged and productive; it also contributes to prosperous societies and a good and sustainable future for all.

Therefore, the need for organisations to include a good, future-proof and clear strategy for health and wellbeing is simply common sense. Such a strategy will be essential for an organisation to thrive and flourish in the years to come.

Disruption and change will be part of the future, and organisations need to prepare their workforce for this reality.

Many organisations have rolled out a strategy addressing the immediate health threat of COVID-19. However, a clear, long-term, future-proof and human-centred approach to health and wellbeing is needed to keep the workforce dynamic, adaptable, engaged and productive in these times of exponential change. An approach that takes into account the immediate and long-term challenges including employability, new working conditions, the use of new technologies, and stress.

Apart from the consequences on our health that COVID-19 has brought along, it is also having a huge impact on employment, with unemployment numbers soaring rapidly. However, this trend is nothing compared to the impact that automation, robotisation and digitisation will have on jobs in the coming years.

In its latest Future of Jobs Report, the World Economic Forum (WEF) projects that by 2025 around 85 million jobs are set to be displaced by automation. Furthermore, according to the Organisation for Economic Co-operation and Development (OECD), a staggering 1 billion jobs, almost one-third of all jobs worldwide, are likely to be transformed by technology in the next decade.

What jobs will be automated?

The extent to which a job is at risk of being automated or robotised can be investigated on replacedbyrobot.info.

The good news is that the WEF also predicts that, despite the accelerated disruption, 97 million new jobs of tomorrow will emerge by 2025. New jobs requiring new core skills. 40% of current work skills are expected to change in the next five years. The most in-demand type of skills of the future will include working with people, problem-solving, technology use and development, and self-management.

New emerging technologies will also bring about new ways of working and new working conditions. This in turn means new challenges for body, mind and spirit. Just as the introduction of the computer led to adverse health conditions such as obesity, cardiovascular disease, eye problems and musculoskeletal pain, mainly due to a more sedentary lifestyle, and certain patterns of social media use have been associated with the development of depression and anxiety.

We can already see how some new emerging technologies are causing new health challenges. For example, some virtual reality (VR) users who wear a headset and engage in full-body, three-dimensional movements are experiencing muscle strain and discomfort.

Rising levels of stress are also a problem. In this fast-changing world, where we will experience ever more rapid demands on ourselves, our way of living and working, the economy and the environment, levels of stress that are already high will rise further. If this added stress continues to be left unmanaged, it will directly and indirectly contribute to even more physical, psychological, social and spiritual (biopsychosocial-spiritual) problems.

Personal Health Responsibility

Health is not a given...

Time will tell what other health problems will emerge when new technologies and new working conditions find their way into work or private life and we start implementing new skills for the emerging jobs and leisure activities. However, organisations can prepare their workforce to become more resilient, adaptable and future-ready. This can be done by including a long-term holistic health, wellbeing and skills training strategy in their strategic plans for the future.

That taking care of employee health and wellbeing has become crucial is evidenced by the list recently published by the WEF of the top 10 skills most in demand for the future, which includes self-management (resilience, stress tolerance and flexibility).

In other words, a life skill where all, on an individual level, take ownership of their health and wellbeing. Health and wellbeing are essential for being able to cope with and rise to the inevitable challenges, problems and setbacks that people will encounter.

Self-management is a life skill that also has a direct and indirect impact on how effective people are in learning and utilising the many hard and soft skills of the future. Just imagine trying to think critically or solve complex problems while depressed or anxious, or preparing a robot when you have acute back pain.

We can learn from the past, without even needing to look towards the future, to see why it is so important to learn self-management. It is sufficient just to observe how the current COVID-19 lockdown, with the ensuing measures of working from home, has led to increased psychosocial risks, technostress, insomnia, conflicts of work-life balance, domestic violence and – due to poor ergonomics – various musculoskeletal disorders. Working from home is not easy, as the conditions are not always optimal. A new remote health and wellbeing strategy is needed, as working from home is here to stay.

I see this in my osteopathy practice on a daily basis: poor working conditions at home are leading to increased musculoskeletal pain and stress. Although teleworking has been forced upon the employee, rarely do I hear of employers taking responsibility for making sure the working conditions at home are optimal or that employees receive support. As a general rule, this is the employer's responsibility. I also see that employees who are working from home have often not really thought it through. Many are working for eight hours or more at the kitchen table without a good chair; some are even working on the sofa or in bed.

With the new working conditions, new training is needed in order for team leaders to be more attentive to health and wellbeing issues emerging in their remote team. In addition, the remote team members need to be trained in how to cope, self-manage and maintain their health and wellbeing while at home.

Health and wellbeing is a shared responsibility, and employers have a front-line role to play here. It is also in their interests, as, for organisations to thrive in a fast-changing world, they need to help their employees become the best version of themselves.

Futurization

Thinking in the present is what has got us here – now it's time to start thinking from the future to get us out of here.

In these fast-changing times, the second life skill that is key to the health and wellbeing of the organisation and its workforce is futurization.

Futurization means incorporating futures thinking into present decisions and choices. In other words, imagining scenarios of what the future will bring or what we would like to see, feel or avoid in the future, and acting upon them today by aligning our decisions and choices to the preferred outcome. This is a change from the current "focus on the present" mindset and helps us to prepare for what is to come. To be mindful of the present can have its benefits, but it does not prepare us for the future. It is also in many ways against our nature, as futures thinking is a ubiquitous feature of the human mind.

In his book *Future Consciousness*, Thomas Lombardo writes that flourishing within the human condition requires a purposeful future focus. Furthermore, he states that, unquestionably, living in the relative present is the fundamental cause behind many of our most significant problems, including global warming.

Our minds, based on millions of years of evolution, are not constructed to live in the present. To evolve, there needs to be anticipation of a general direction for the future. It is the nature of the conscious human mind that we act with purpose and perceive with anticipation.

Dr Bob Johansen, a futurist with the Institute for the Future (IFTF), explains that what you need in the middle of a crisis is a North Star that gives you clarity. It is often easier to look 10 years ahead than to look one or two years ahead, especially in a crisis.

What the brain wants is certainty – and when the immediate future is difficult to predict, as it is today, we can achieve greater clarity by thinking in the longer term.

Futurizing health and wellbeing means proactively thinking of the long-term aspirations for your health and wellbeing (motivation). It is creating an image of a preferred future, of the way you want to feel 5–10 years from now. On an organisational level, it is thinking how you want your employees to feel 5–10 years from now.

The future is influenced by y'our decisions, choices and actions. Therefore, on both accounts, when we align our behaviour in the present to the preferred future, we create clarity that will help us navigate uncertainty.

Helping employees to futurize themselves, empowering them to shift towards futures thinking and conscious navigation into the future – from the future, and on purpose – will also enhance their personal health responsibility. It can also become a great motivator for adapting to new, more digital ways of working and preparing for the changes to come.

Conclusion

Futurize y'our human capital

We are living in a fast-changing and challenging world. A world where COVID-19, new emerging technologies and climate change are challenging organisations and the workforce to discover how to futurize themselves to stay relevant, engaged and productive.

Fostering health and wellbeing is critical in order for individuals to cope with and flourish through these changes, as well as for organisations to thrive.

The wealth of business is best founded on the health of its workers, and investing in health and wellbeing is a responsibility.

However, organisations and their employees struggle with the practical implementation of health and wellbeing within the new conditions.

In these fast-changing times, creating a good future where employees flourish and organisations thrive requires a new holistic and future-minded collaborative approach to health and wellbeing.

A new approach that hinges not only on biopsychosocial and spiritual (purpose) aspects to accommodate the individual and organisational needs but also on the requisite life skills, personal health responsibility and futurization.

Personal health responsibility is needed to enhance the

employees' ability to adapt and self-manage, especially while working from home. This skill is not only in the interests of the individual but also in the interests of organisations, which will need people who can access the best part of themselves and thrive while working conditions are changing.

Employers can enhance the health and wellbeing of their employees by identifying people's needs, evaluating the existing policies, and accelerating innovative solutions. This should go hand in hand with offering the coaching and training needed for employees to take responsibility for maintaining their own health.

Futurization is needed to prepare employees for the future and for flourishing in the flow of evolution.

Shifting towards incorporating futures thinking and conscious navigation into the future – from the future, on purpose – will also enhance and reinforce personal health responsibility.

In the same way that successful organisations futurize themselves by imagining future scenarios upon which they act in the present, so employees must be encouraged to futurize themselves to stay healthy and relevant in a fast-changing world.

Health and wellbeing is a shared responsibility, but appropriately empowering employees can help them become the best version of themselves – which in turn increases employee engagement and potential – reduces costs and helps to ensures that the business will thrive in an uncertain future. Ensuring healthier lives and promoting wellbeing will also contribute to a more sustainable future and more prosperous societies.

Change affects us all differently, but one thing is for sure: change is stressful, and lots of change over a very short period of time can, over time, have severe consequences for your health, wellbeing and future.

But I hope you see why I'm concerned for your health, wellbeing and future, knowing that over the next 10 years more change is expected than in the previous 100 years. Over the next 20 years – so still in our lifetime for most of us – humanity will change more than in the previous 300 years! (Gerd Leonhard) That is a lot of change and a hell of a lot of stress – and stress is already one of the biggest health problems worldwide.

The key to navigating that is resilience.

But what is stress–resilience?

The best antidote to stress is resilience... having the ability to respond to change or adversity proactively and resourcefully.

Lauren Mackler

As described before, resilience is y'our ability to adapt and/or bounce back from adversity and return to ease (reaset). It's getting up when you fall, it's muscles that contract and then relax. On an emotional level, it is the capacity to bounce back and get over – and move on after – a conflict or a setback.

Resilience can also be seen as your ability to maintain or regain stability, despite experiencing adversity.

In my practice, I have a Toroflux® to illustrate what resilience is. A Toroflux® is a kinetic spring toy for children made from one ribbon of steel which is woven into a doughnut-shaped torus. When it is unfolded and you press on it lightly (stress), it will change shape and when you release the pressure on it, it will go back to its original toroidal form (resilience). However, if you keep pressing on it (chronic stress) or give it a strong push (acute stress), it will collapse, fold into itself and will not be able to go back to its original shape without help. Look it up on my website www.osteopathbrussels.com or on YouTube and you'll see what I mean.

> **Resources**, according to the Oxford Dictionary of English, are: i. A stock or supply of money, materials, staff, and other assets that can be drawn on by a person or organisation in order to function effectively. ii. An action or strategy which may be adopted in adverse circumstances.

Chapter 3: A Resilient Future

If resilience is your ability to bounce back from adversity, chronic stress occurs when these same demands outweigh your resources. Over time, chronic stress will be harmful for your health and wellbeing. It will change your time perspective, change your behaviour and shorten your lifespan.

Stress in itself is not the problem. Stress is, after all, a natural biological and behavioural response to a real or imagined threat called a stressor (demand). Examples of stressors can be a wild animal that is chasing you or a car that is racing towards you. But a stressor can also be a loud noise, a smell, a chemical product in the air, a robot that has replaced you at work, a heatwave, changes due to climate change, a pandemic, a cyberattack or a fight with your partner. Not all stressors are negative in nature. A new job, moving house, a raise in salary, a holiday, getting married, learning a new skill and futurizing yourself can be considered as stressors. Anything that asks you to adapt can be seen as a stressor.

Stress is a physiological process to maintain stability through change. "Tom, stability through change – I think you mentioned that before." I did, didn't I, a few pages back when I spoke about allostasis.

> Sterling and Eyer (1988) defined **allostasis** as the set of mind–body systemic events aimed at regulating the recovery from stress.

When you encounter a threatening or life-changing situation, your body will respond with a series of neuro-hormonal changes that help you to cope. For example, these internal changes can give you a burst of energy so you're able to fight off attackers, or increase oxygen to the brain and improve attention, focus, energy and determination when you're studying for an exam. So, some stress is healthy and helpful – as long as you are resilient and are able to bounce back when the danger, real or not, or the extra demand on you is over.

However, chronic or excessive stress can lead to allostatic load. This occurs when your stress response can't reaset because the demands on your body were higher than its resources to bounce back and dysautonomia (the dysregulation of the autonomic nervous system) sets in.

> **Stress-related dysautonomia** is the dysregulation of the autonomic nervous system and occurs when the body is essentially in a sympathetic state constantly. This is a state of the body where the stress response is constantly firing and is unable to return to ease and activate the rest and digest response.

Over time this can lead to you having a combination of different symptoms like neck, shoulder and back pain, cardiovascular and digestive problems, immune deficiency, behavioural changes, insomnia, memory problems, and it can even change the structure of your brain. Ouch! These in turn can lead to or aggravate other health problems like cancer, Alzheimer's or Crohn's disease, diabetes, anxiety, depression and burnout.

> According to the Polyvagal Theory (Porges, 2011), the common thread and rationale behind dysautonomia is that

chronic or excessive stress leads to a surge in the activity of the dorsal branch and the shutdown of the activity of the ventral branch of the vagus nerve (evolutionarily newer part) and you regress to an earlier, more primitive evolutionary response of either spinal sympathetic activity (flight/fight) or depressive behaviour (withdrawal).

(Rosenberg, 2017)

As you can probably imagine by now, stress – although essential to help you get away quickly from an oncoming car – can, in the long term, actually become a stressor in itself! This ain't what you want when you are trying to envisage a good life and a GREAT future.

A fast-changing world will mean lots of change, which means lots of stress. How you cope with the increased levels of stress will define your future.

SIDELINE REFLECTION:

Isn't it interesting that all the aforementioned multi-system chronic stress-related symptoms are experienced by people suffering from long COVID?! My experience working with patients who have chronic stress or long COVID is that, so far, all have benefited nearly instantly from the osteopathy-based Reaset Approach that I developed.

Info from the NHS and CDC on long COVID

For some people, coronavirus (COVID-19) can cause symptoms that last weeks or months after the infection has gone. This is sometimes called post-COVID-19 syndrome or "long COVID".

About long COVID

How long it takes to recover from COVID-19 is different for everybody. Many people feel better in a few days or weeks, and most will make a full recovery within 12 weeks. But for some people, symptoms can last longer. The chances of having long-term symptoms does not seem to be linked to how ill you are when you first get COVID-19. People who had mild symptoms at first can still have long-term problems.

Common chronic stress and long COVID symptoms include:

- Joint or muscle pain
- Extreme tiredness (fatigue)
- Difficulty sleeping (insomnia)
- Headaches, back pains, stomach problems and diarrhoea
- Heart palpitations
- Problems with memory and concentration
- Depression and anxiety
- Dizziness
- Changes in breath rate
- Chest pain or tightness
- Tinnitus, earaches

Other long COVID symptoms

- Post-exertional malaise
- Brain fog

- Pins and needles
- Feeling sick, stomach aches, loss of appetite
- Changes to sense of smell or taste

Not all challenges are signs to change

Difficulties strengthen the mind, as labour does the body.

Seneca

Before I go on, you need to know that not all challenges are signs to change. Some challenges make you stronger and bring you closer to your goal. For example, learning new skills can be challenging. Staying home during a lockdown, not being able to visit friends or family, can be challenging. Athletes training for years to be on top of their game for the next Olympics is challenging. Writing a book is challenging, but it doesn't get written by sitting on the sofa watching TV.

Exams are extremely challenging and can seem to stop your flow experience. I remember very well how I struggled for all my osteopathy exams. When I was studying, I was swimming against the current for months, and faster currents would push me under the water, but I kept swimming. But these challenges were there for a reason, were part of my evolution to becoming an osteopath. Oh yes, I cursed, cried, questioned if this hardship was all worth it and was truly leading me to what I had envisaged becoming. But each time, the answer was yes. I wanted and needed this. It mattered, and I needed to take the therapist in me into a specific direction. A direction that was more recognised than – but in line with – kinesiology, where I would feel more whole and could use all my newly discovered faculties. Osteopathy was that direction, and it fitted my personal profile to a T. So in moments of doubt, I reconnected with my future as a therapist in the form of an osteopath, which gave me the resilience, the motivation and the stamina to go on.

This type of motivation or stamina is no different from the motivation and extra energy you get when thinking of your upcoming holiday when you are having an awful day at work. This pre-holiday happiness or energy booster can be experienced weeks or even months before the holiday actually begins – fantastic, right? I thought so when I started to use this analogy to explain the futures effect to my patients.

When I used the holiday example, everybody recognised what I meant immediately but had never thought about it before. For some patients, this fried their circuits a bit. They completely got it on a deeper level, but when trying to apply it, their brain couldn't process it. I noticed that most of the time, these were patients who – to manage their stress – had been practising mindfulness for years.

"Mindfulness is the energy of being aware and awake to the present moment. It is the continuous practice of touching life deeply in every moment of daily life. To be mindful is to be truly alive, present, and at one with those around you and with what you are doing" (Thich Nhat Hanh).

While mindfulness is all about bringing your attention to the present moment, it doesn't mean one should deny the future. I often see that practitioners lose sight of this, and forget to be mindful of their future.

To be mindful means that you are not in your default mode. The default mode is, for example, when you open your wallet at the checkout of your local supermarket to pay for the groceries you'd wanted to make that surprise dinner, are surprised to see that your wallet is empty and can't remember where you've spent the €50 that you are sure was in it that morning. If you had been more aware during the day, you wouldn't even be checking for the money – you'd go straight for the debit card.

To be mindful can also be in relation to future events. Futurizing yourself to evolve on purpose is not done on autopilot but consciously, and for that, you have to be mindful.

> The fact is that practising mindfulness can actually help you in envisaging your future, as it helps to reduce stress. Remember that stress over time can lead to anxiety and depression, mood changes, memory problems and changes in time perception.
>
> Therefore, it is imperative when you want to futurize yourself or to practise any other form of future-oriented awareness and planning, including for business purposes, that you do it in a state of ease. Practising mindfulness can help with this, but if you feel it doesn't bring you back to ease, get professional help that includes the reasetting of the autonomic nervous system.

The past has come and gone, and the present might be the only place that exists. However, if you aspire to have a GREAT future, you need to spend time being mindful of the future. "The present is always leaving, and the future is always arriving. We have the power to greatly influence the future by consciously making present-moment choices that are consistent with the future we want" (Vilhauer, 2014).

Just living in the present moment is in many ways against our nature, as futures thinking is a ubiquitous feature of the human mind. Based on millions of years of evolution, our minds are not constructed to live in the present. To evolve, there needs to be anticipation of a general direction for the future (Lombardo, 2017).

This has been so since conception. A fertilised human egg cell develops into a human and never a chicken because it has direction. As it were, a design is realised.

To my patients, I often illustrate how much futures thinking or anticipation is ingrained in us by explaining: "My stomach is a futurist. As soon as it sees chocolate, it starts a digestive process in preparation for that first bite. It anticipates what is coming, just like my mouth that starts salivating."

Imagine our digestive system not doing that. Imagine if our body didn't anticipate danger. Life wouldn't be as we know it.

Looking to the future has always defined humanity; it is part of our DNA. Your brain is an anticipation machine, but so is your body. The fact that we are still here is thanks to our ability to anticipate.

The uniquely human ability to visualise and to time travel in our minds allows us to anticipate consciously just like my stomach does autonomously, and to intentionally shape and control our future through our deliberate behaviour. That, in turn, makes us more resilient, because we become better prepared (Suddendorf et al., 2016).

At any time, we can start to visualise. Nothing can stop us time travelling – not even a crisis. For example, during a pandemic where the immediate future is difficult to predict, we can turn to this innate ability by taking ownership of our long-term future, envisioning what we truly want, and using that vision to steer our actions and gain control over the present.

Thus, the future becomes a fantastic stress management tool

and a great asset to y'our health and wellbeing. The future does not exist except in our mind, but unlike the past, we can change it, give it a direction by aligning our decisions, choices and actions. I know this might be a concept that needs getting used to, but you'll find very quickly that it has merit. Although futurizing yourself means aligning and committing yourself to long-term objectives, you don't have to wait to feel or see the benefits. Some (not all – that would be too amazing) are immediate, because the decisions and choices you make and the actions you take to realise the future are in the present. Remember what I explained about the benefits of planning your holiday or just thinking about it? I would even go further and claim that sometimes the stage of planning and thinking about your holiday is more joyous than the holiday itself. The future is now; this is what is so fantastic about it.

Matthew Killingsworth, senior fellow at the Wharton School at the University of Pennsylvania, says: "As humans, we spend a lot of our mental lives living in the future and our future-mindedness can be a source of joy if we know good things are coming, and travel is an especially good thing to have to look forward to."

(Jackson Curran, 2020)

The future as a milestone

Direction is more important than speed. We are so busy looking at our speedometers that we forget the milestone.

Author unknown

Another great benefit of futurizing yourself is that at any moment you can evaluate your progress. It can also help you progress in challenging times.

While evolving on purpose, I reconnected with my future at regular intervals. Sometimes this was a conscious decision; on other occasions, it was a tool I used when I faced resistance, when things were not going so smoothly any more.

I have learned that when I become aware that I'm experiencing a challenging moment – which often goes hand in hand with stress, discontentment and unease – I need to ask the question: "What is happening?" – "Why am I feeling this or that…?"

Am I feeling this because I've deviated from my path, or is it helping me to grow stronger and bring me closer to my goal – my preferred future? If I didn't know where I was going, how could or can I know the difference?

It makes me think of a Delft plate that was hanging above the kitchen table in my childhood home: "God, grant me the serenity to accept the things I cannot change, courage to change the things I can, and wisdom to know the difference." One day I must ask my parents why they had this hanging there and what it meant to them. In any case, it left an impression on me.

The question I want to ask here is: "What wisdom do you need to know the difference?" In other words, what knowledge or experience do you need to be able to make an informed decision?

And this makes me think back to Thomas Lombardo's words: "We create a good future, defined as flourishing in the flow of evolution, through the heightening of future consciousness, which is achieved by developing a core set of character virtues, most notably and centrally wisdom."

For me, it is clear that knowing what the future you want and are evolving into is very wise. I might not go as far as saying "He who has a why to live for can bear almost any how" (Friedrich Nietzsche) but yes, something like that.

So, coming back to my experience of reconnecting with my future as an osteopath to help me bear the many demands, it worked for me. Exams were part of the journey of becoming an osteopath, and that they had stopped my flow was only an illusion. Underlying dynamics were going on that were needed to make me stronger and achieve what I had set out to realise.

Rehearse your future

If the latest research on epigenetics tells us that the environment signals the gene, and the end product from an experience in the environment is an emotion, as we embrace the emotion ahead of the environment, we are signalling the gene ahead of the environment.

Joe Dispenza

I'd like to share the story of how I approached my final exam from the future. This was an exam where I had to examine a patient while three examiners were looking on.

The five years I had been studying osteopathy were very challenging. As a very slow learner, I was always one step behind and unable to really integrate all that we had learned. A fact that hadn't gone unnoticed by my teachers.

However, at the final clinical exam, where I had 20 minutes to examine a patient and determine a treatment strategy, something happened. I had practised for this exam with Clara, a fellow osteopathy student. She had finished her theoretical exam a few years before me but still needed to do the clinical exam. When D-day came, we were as ready as we could be. Still, exams are stressful, and waiting for my turn was nerve-racking, to say the least.

However, as soon as I entered the examination room, I felt calm. I felt the room was mine, and when I was told what was expected of me, I started examining the patient.

I don't remember how long into the examination it was when one of the three examiners, who had seemingly become a bit impatient, said something like: "Hurry up, Tom, you don't have all day." A question and tone that could easily have destabilised me but left me completely unfazed. I was in the flow zone, completely absorbed by what I was doing. The room was mine, and it felt like nothing, not even the examiners, could touch me. I looked at the clock; I was still within my allotted time, so I continued to examine the patient at my pace. Just before the 20 minutes were over, I said I was ready.

I explained to two of the three examiners, who had also been my teachers for the past five years, what I had found. I can't recall my exact words, but something like: "I feel there is a tension between…" and I showed them the back of the head and under the sacrum. I continued to tell them, while demonstrating with my hands, what I would do to release that condition. Then they started grilling me.

I don't know for how long I was grilled like this. Also, I did not really understand their questions – what they were after – until the third examiner, an osteopath I didn't know, shouted to his colleagues to stop. I'm not exaggerating; he shouted to the two others: "Stop! He has given the correct answer, hasn't he? So why question him further?" I'll never forget that moment. I think the examiners were as perplexed by the outburst as I was. They stopped immediately, and I could leave the room. I was asked to go back in only after all the other students had done their clinical exams. I had no idea if I had passed or not. It all went so fast – and that abrupt stop, I didn't know what to think about it.

So there I was, standing in front of a tribunal of three judges to receive my sentence. I was less confident this time when I was in the room, but I didn't need to worry: I had passed. Yeah! It turned out that the reason they had grilled me was that they wanted me to use the terminology for the condition I had described: a craniosacral compression. Oh boy… of course!

However, what I had differentiated and the treatment protocol I had offered was exactly what they were looking for. They were pleasantly surprised by what they had seen me do. If there was one student they thought was going to fail, it was me. They told me so and thus were very surprised, and their praise of my progress was so much more sincere and touching.

The student most unlikely to pass had passed with high marks from the examiners! The only one of the dozen that had started five years earlier that actually did and passed his clinical exam and went on to get a diploma, a bachelor's and a master's in osteopathy.

But how did I end up in that flow state?

No, it was not by coincidence. I had rehearsed that future over and over again in my mind every day for a week. Every day I took time out to sit down and close my eyes to first practise a heart coherence breathing technique to calm me and then to envisage myself entering the building the exam was held, then the room, seeing the examiners and creating in my mind and body a feeling of harmony and calm. Every day I projected myself into my future in this way. I had studied. I knew how to do the protocol, but I wanted to feel in control in that stressful moment. When I actually entered the room, that room was mine.

This was an extraordinary experience for me and another example of how you can benefit by embracing and using the future.

After passing my clinical exam, if you had told me that I would one day have a master's in osteopathy, I would have laughed at you. A master's in osteopathy didn't even exist back then, and I still thought I wasn't clever enough for a university degree. But I did go on to do my BSc, and I got my MSc in osteopathy just before my 49th birthday.

What I want to get to with these stories is that when you are on a personal evolution learning or growing curve, you will face resistance. When you are fulfilling your destiny, you will face resistance. Resistance is part of the processes when evolving on purpose.

When faced with resistance, stop and ask yourself the question: Is it because I deviated from my path, or is it for me to grow? You can only answer this question when you have designed or, in other words, defined a future you want to grow into. If you haven't got a clear image of how you want to feel and/or who you want to evolve into, maybe this is the time to think about it – the time to make space for your future.

Let me repeat this: You have a measure of control over your future through your decisions, choices and actions – your behaviour. Therefore, futurizing yourself or choosing a future before a future is chosen for you, and incorporating it into your decisions, choices and actions, is a means to influence your future.

As a body-centred stress coach, I would like to give you one more futurizing health and wellbeing tip: "Mind your body before your body reminds you!" The body is the vehicle of your future.

So, make sure you give yourself enough time to relax, rest and recuperate, and ask for help in time – especially in challenging moments. You are like an athlete on a quest to become a better version of yourself. Athletes know this – and they know that to get stronger and better, they will need to push themselves to achieve their goal, and know when to stop and take a break to rest.

We all need something to look forward to in life

Don't let life stand in the way of your future.

Tom Meyers

Let's dig a bit deeper into taking ownership of your long-term future when the immediate future is difficult to predict.

At the time I am writing this book, we are living in the midst of the COVID-19 pandemic. In March 2020, life suddenly changed. Who would have thought then that two years later we would still not be back to normal or that we would never return to the normal that was? For many people, this has been, and will continue to be for some time to come, a very stressful time personally and economically.

As governments introduce new rules, and regulations change every week to keep on top of the pandemic, it has even become harder to think and plan ahead. The toll of this volatile, uncertain, complex and ambiguous time on body, mind and spirit is something I see in my patients all too often.

I also see that patients and people around me are becoming more and more fixated on the present. A good example is that some are still working at the kitchen table instead of investing in a good chair or other ergonomic equipment for work to support their body and reduce the health risks associated with bad posture. Reduced exercise is another consequence of this pandemic that has so many people working from home.

Those who had an outdoor exercise routine keep doing it. However, those who didn't or went to the gym, yoga class, or just had their daily exercise going to work or at work by walking from meeting to meeting, stopped exercising altogether during the lockdown.

Patients often tell me they know they are not moving enough as they rarely go out of the house, but they hadn't thought ahead to consider the consequences. That type of short-sightedness lands them in my practice with neck, shoulder and/or back pain, increased stress or other physical or psychological issues.

That we have difficulties planning ahead today is, of course, understandable. The future is very uncertain at the moment and very dependent on the evolution of the pandemic. It is also dependent on the loosening of the restrictions set by respective governments.

The pandemic is a current crisis, but it is not the only crisis in which it is difficult to plan ahead or think of the future. In any kind of crisis that affects us, we can become fixated on the present. I know this all too well from personal experience.

Again, I urge you to think about your own situation and what the future you want. How do you want to feel when this pandemic is under control? You want to feel healthy? Then you need to take care of yourself today. Make sure you exercise enough, have a balanced diet, take regular breaks, stay in contact with family and friends – even if that means online. Set up a dedicated workspace and get the right equipment so you can also work in optimal conditions at home. Set boundaries – and, whatever you do, be good to you.

Rewiring the brain for the future

The human brain now holds the key to our future. We have to recall the image of the planet from outer space: a single entity in which air, water, and continents are interconnected. That is our home.

David Suzuki

Taking ownership of your long-term future needs to be done on purpose. Earlier in this book, I mentioned that your body and brain are wired for anticipation and that this is mostly so for the immediate and short-term future. When it comes to the long-term future, it is a whole different story.

I could give you the solution to overcome your evolutionary limitations straight away, but I'm a firm believer that understanding the problem and what needs to happen to integrate long-term futures thinking into your routine is far more powerful than giving it to you on a plate.

I also believe in your genius and ingenuity to come up with solutions when you know the problem to overcome. That optimism and belief in human empowerment stems from years of working with patients on their stress management. So let me try to explain a bit about what goes on in the wondrous world of your brain, and talk a bit about where things get processed. This is important to know when you want to adopt a futures mindset and make the future an asset to your health, wellbeing and then some.

Let's start with the cognitive abilities that you will need in order to think about the future. Cognitive abilities are orchestrated in the forebrain, also called the prefrontal cortex. Play with me here and put your hand on your forehead, the area of your face above your eyebrows. Don't be shy. Put your hand on your forehead, close your eyes, and breathe in and out slowly. In your hand, behind skin, skull, and three protective membranes, lies the part of your brain called the prefrontal cortex, or PFC for short.

Now, how does it make you feel when you just hold your hand there and breathe in and out slowly? Relaxing, right?!

By the way, have you ever wondered why you tap or rub your forehead when you have forgotten a name during a conversation? Or why you instinctively hold your forehead when your child or baby is in distress? Keep reading for an answer.

As I mentioned before, stress can, in specific circumstances, impair cognitive functioning, functions that take place in the prefrontal cortex.

The second thing to know is that stress can strengthen certain emotions, like fear and anxiety, and make you fall back to more primitive conditioned responses to certain habits or routines. These are steered by another part of your brain, called the amygdala (Arnsten, 2009).

The amygdalae (there are two of them) are situated behind the eyes at the height of your temples. The temples are those soft spots on the left and right sides of your face behind and above the cheekbones. They are the part of your head that you instinctively rub when you have tension stress. Maybe you can ponder about why you do this, too.

Anyway, knowing that stress has these inhibitory effects on the one hand, and activating effects on the other, it shouldn't come as a surprise that prolonged stress – experienced, for example, during a long-term pandemic – is not without its consequences for your thinking, emotions and mental state.

A word of clarification: it is, of course, not stress itself that is the problem, but the cascade of neuro-hormonal and physiological changes (with a big role for adrenaline and cortisol) stimulated through stress that will become a nuisance and impact your physical, mental, social and spiritual health and wellbeing. It is just a matter of time, conditions and, among other factors, your personality and proactive coping strategies.

The impact on your cognitive abilities (concentration, anticipation, learning, memorisation, etc.) and emotions (fear, anxiety, etc.), that you are a bit more short-tempered and/or anxious after long periods of stress, probably has something to do with the fact that, over time, prolonged stress – due to neuro-hormonal and vascular changes – will shrink the prefrontal cortex and another part of the brain called the hippocampus (Arnsten, 2009). Yes, you read that correctly: chronic stress shrinks parts of your brain. Ouch!

The hippocampus, a U-shaped structure in the brain with the amygdalae at the front, plays an important role in some emotions, learning, and the consolidation of information from short-term memory to long-term memory. A reduced hippocampus is associated with poorer memory and impairments in mental time travel.

While the PFC and the hippocampus are shrinking, some parts of your brain increase in volume. Those parts that are linked to your immediate survival, that make you more alert for danger, like the amygdalae. Yes, those almond-shaped clusters of nuclei located behind your eyes at the level of the temples and that are situated at each end of the "U" of the hippocampus. These almond-shaped clusters will increase in volume.

"What does the amygdalae do?" you may ask. It plays an important role in emotions, behaviour, and the processing of fear. A larger amygdala means you and your brain will become more receptive to stress, and the future becomes an even more dangerous place. When you become more receptive to stress, that means you become more fearful, including fearful about the future. You also become more anxious and irrational and start to say or buy things that you later regret.

I think we've all been there, done that and got the proverbial T-shirt. At least I have.

All that said, I think you can start to see or at least imagine that, for the promotion of futures thinking, planning, and decision-making, stress is not your friend.

By the way, chronic stress is also not what you want to have during a pandemic or health crisis, as it will suppress your immune system. This book is not about the latter aspect of stress, so I won't go into the details. However, as a future-minded and education-oriented osteopath and body-centred stress coach, I do feel the need to mention it, and I want you to take stress and its many consequences seriously. A well-informed woman or man is worth two. "Mind your body before your body reminds you" is my philosophy.

Now here is another titbit of information that is interesting to know: Although your body is a primordial futurist and perfect for anticipating what is going to happen next, your brain is naturally really terrible at thinking about the long-term future. For example, when you think of your future self, 10 years from now, something quirky happens – an unexpected glitch in your brain. Studies suggest that your brain starts acting as if you're thinking about a stranger, someone you don't know very well, when you imagine your future self. When the future you is someone you don't know very well, why would you care for it? The more your future self feels like a stranger – that is, the more disconnected you are from your future self – the less motivated you will be to plan for your future (Hershfield, 2011).

When I read about this phenomenon, which has been corroborated with functional brain scans (fMRI scans), I wondered if this glitch could be considered as a reason why, for example, smokers keep smoking while they must be aware by now that nearly 9 out of 10 lung cancer deaths are caused by smoking cigarettes: "Cancer?! It will not happen to me, as me in the future is not me!" so to speak.

And what exactly is this glitch? Well, there is increased activity in the mPFC of your brain when you think about yourself and decreased activation when you think of others. The same decrease happens in the mPFC when you think of your future self. It's a gradual process, meaning that, the further into the future you go, the less activity there is in the mPFC and the more you become a stranger to yourself – and the less likely you are to make informed choices for long-term benefits (McGonigal, 2017).

"What's mPFC, Tom? Does the PFC stand for prefrontal cortex as you mentioned before when you were talking about stress?" Indeed it does, and the "m" stands for medial, that part of the brain nearest to the midline.

Pure speculation on my part here, but could it be that thinking of your future self causes a stress response?

Luckily for you and others, you have a measure of control over your quirky brain, and you can – on purpose – counteract this outdated evolutionary trait. You might already want to start reflecting on what you can do to make the future you your best friend, an ally you feel closely bonded to.

Anyway, I hope, with this very brief introduction to some of the key players, you have an idea of why you might have difficulty planning ahead in a crisis or thinking about your future – and who or what to blame for it. It's your brain. But you are not powerless: your brain is full of potential that you can explore to overcome a crisis by rewiring it.

Making your future self your best friend

Thinking about the future is daunting, but there is no time like the present to think about it.

Tom Meyers

So what do you need to do to make your future you you, and turn a stressor like futures thinking into an asset? You need to… futurize yourself! (I think you saw that one coming…) Futurizing yourself over time rewires your brain.

Spend time familiarising yourself with your future, the stressor, the stranger. "Tom, are you saying that I need to make the future me my best friend?" Exactly – I couldn't have said it better. If natural evolution won't do the job in time, help yourself to evolve on purpose. Make the future you your best friend. In essence, it's as simple as that.

OK, I'm exaggerating a bit – and I do realise that, if you are currently struggling to survive, this ain't so easy. The first three levels of Maslow's pyramid of needs do need to be met. Were they met when I started futurizing myself? Luckily, they were, now that I reflect on it.

Sitting at my desk at the back of my failing shop, I was safe. I still had a roof over my head; I still had food to eat and water to drink. For how long, I didn't know, but at that moment I was OK. This is probably why I was able to think and reflect when I needed to answer the questions I was given, even though my stress response was, without a doubt, very active at the time.

Developing a resilient future

Change is the law of life. And those who look only to the past or the present are certain to miss the future.

John F. Kennedy

The future as a tool for stress management and resilience building. You might not have thought about it before reading this book, but I'm pretty sure you are doing it already in your life. You've planned a holiday before, right? How did the planning or thinking about your holiday make you feel on a particularly stressful day? Do you have insurance? Do you save money in an account for a rainy day? Why? Why do you brush your teeth?

These are all examples of where you are acting today to prevent something in the future. In other words, you've thought about possible future scenarios and are implementing strategies to prevent something like bad teeth or to make conditions for the future better, like saving for a rainy day. These are all forms of stress management, in my humble opinion.

So yes, futures thinking, creating future scenarios or making plans for the future is something we do, and it is good for us, for you. We just haven't applied it to other parts of our life where it could be of use, because, in the past, times, needs and circumstances were different.

But with our environment changing fast and the consequences this has and will have further on our lives, including the survival of humanity, we have no time to lose.

Futurizing yourself is key for your health and wellbeing and will help you become more resilient in times of change and adversity. Imagine an astronaut going to the International Space

Station, and there is an emergency. If they hadn't trained to stay calm and collected – if they hadn't trained with hundreds of scenarios, how do you think they would fare?

If you are a taxi driver, and you haven't reskilled and suddenly find yourself without a job because all taxis have become automated, how will you feel? What will be the consequences for your family, your children? How will you feel when you suddenly find yourself feet deep in water as global warming has caused sea levels to rise? Did you know that paradises like Seychelles, Maldives, Tuvalu and Kiribati will be mostly underwater within the next 50 to 100 years? The same fate, over time, awaits New York, Sydney, Venice, Amsterdam, and so many other coastal regions.

Oh, you are still thinking that it will not happen to you? That it only happens to others... Remember what I said earlier about the glitch in your brain that makes you believe that the future you isn't you while in reality, it is you. A global pandemic was also happening to others. Yeah, like you were living on another planet, Tom. Yes, I had to learn this important lesson too, the hard way. That what I thought was "a show far from my bed" (as we say in Dutch) was happening to me.

Futurizing yourself, making the future a friend by practising incorporating futures thinking into y'our decisions, choices and actions is the mindshift we need to evolve on purpose to flourish and thrive. Futurizing yourself without delay is the key to get what the future – which I hope you have conceived by now – you want.

I was in a business and life crisis when I was told to think about the future. When my business was failing and the walls were closing in on me, it was the question to imagine an ideal day in

10 years' time – the question that made me design the future I wanted – that saved me and would help me to flourish and thrive over the next 20 years.

Yes, at first when I was asked to ponder upon this question, my reaction was rejection. How was it possible to think about an ideal and brighter future while my problems were here today and needed to be fixed now, not tomorrow? How was it possible to imagine beauty when there was so much darkness around me?

Now, looking back over the past 20 years and all that has transpired, I know that it is thanks to that one question that I am what I am today. The answer gave me a focal point based on which I could pull myself out of my misery.

"And what about the other questions you mentioned in your previous book? The questions that helped you put a new light on your past and finding your potential. Weren't they decisive in the process too?" They were important preparatory steps, and without them, I wouldn't have been able to come up with the appropriate answer. But what's the use of knowing how to look at the world or knowing your potential and then stopping there? By imagining my ideal day, I gave my life meaning and a direction, a sense and a purpose. Something to aim for, a direction to go in, and a reason for doing so. Together, they gave me resolve and determination I hadn't experienced before. I was going to live and fulfil my destiny and evolve into the best version of myself.

Meditation masters might promote living in the moment and focusing on the present to manage stress, but this will not help you prevent stress from happening if you lose your job and hadn't foreseen it. So yes, what do you know?! I know it might sound bonkers, but thinking about the future will build resilience. It will help you to prevent stress, and also to weather stress by proactively focusing on a long-term "YOU" project. By scanning the horizon and seeing demands or opportunities in the distant future to which you can align your decisions, choices and actions in the ongoing present to meet these demands and opportunities in the future.

Or you can anticipate what might happen and get ahead of change by futurizing yourself. That is, preparing yourself beforehand, thus before a crisis or change emerges in the case of our taxi driver. By now, a taxi driver must have heard that the likelihood that their job will be automated in the near future is very high. Exactly when this will be is unknown. We can't predict the future with certainty; we can only create scenarios or anticipate what will happen. That all forms of transport are going to be automated is beyond question. Again, have a look at replacedbyrobot.info to find out what the likelihood is. While there, maybe you want to check your own job. Anyway, if driving a taxi doesn't get automated soon, we might have more serious problems to tackle – but let's stay optimistic.

OK, let's suppose you are a taxi driver; you might not think that losing your job is optimistic, but this is evolution, and evolution is an undeniable reality and part of life. Remember that the horse and cart were replaced by cars – and what took 50 years then will take about five years now. Be ready for it!

Here's my advice if you are a taxi driver, cashier, meter reader, fast-food worker, telemarketer, loan officer or radiologist (to name but a few): I suggest you proactively start learning a new skill if you don't want to find yourself in a crisis when it happens.

Everything that can be automated will be automated

The central question of 2025 will be: What are people for in a world that does not need their labor, and where only a minority are needed to guide the 'bot-based economy?

Stowe Boyd

According to estimates by the Organisation for Economic Co-operation and Development (OECD), more than one billion jobs – that's almost one-third of all jobs worldwide – are likely to be transformed by technology in the next decade (WEF, 2020). Transformed meaning that some jobs will be lost and for others reskilling or upskilling is needed.

The good thing for those that lose their jobs is that new jobs and opportunities will be created. The World Economic Forum (WEF) predicts that despite the accelerated disruption to jobs, there will be an overall net positive between job growth and actual decline (WEF, 2022). That said, these new jobs and opportunities will require new skills, of course.

To have a GREAT future, make sure you become resilient for the futures to come. Inform yourself, anticipate and prevent change from becoming a stressor through your decisions, choices and actions. In other words, futurize yourself by starting to scan the horizon and taking action proactively. You can start today by analysing the demands and opportunities these changes will bring, and reflect on what you can do today to be ready when these demands are needed or the opportunities have emerged. You can also develop a strategy based on what will not change and build on that. This is an interesting approach adopted by Jeff Bezos (Aton, 2020) that I mentioned earlier.

Until now, we have been primarily reactive when it comes to

change, which has been OK in a slow-changing world. However, that world ain't no more. We live in a fast-changing world where we need to be proactive if we want to stay relevant and resilient.

CEOs and managers of thriving businesses know this. They have scanned the horizon and created scenarios for the future, and plans to adapt to each and every one of them.

Others, like Elon Musk or Jeff Bezos, are busy creating the demands of the future. Now we, and I mean all 8 billion of us, have to come to terms with this. We have to come to terms with ourself. We need to look within and acknowledge that the world around us has changed, and we need to get an overview of our place in the world of tomorrow. We are ready for this. You can do this.

Design your life on purpose

Don't ask: What is the purpose of my life – of living? Instead, ask yourself: What purpose do I want to give my life so that it is worth living?

Tom Meyers

In my book *Futurize Yourself – Design your life on purpose*, I weave my personal journey and the lessons I have learned together with details of how and why you should consider doing the same. Today, I still use the same questions and the same mindset to create my futures. Yes, I scan the horizon.

Yes, I checked the replacedbyrobot.info website. I was curious and needed to know. As an osteopath, I'm pretty safe, apparently. The likelihood that my job or any other manual healing approach will be replaced is close to nil.

However, what will happen when nanobots arrive? Nanobots that can be injected into your bloodstream and flow through your body to detect disease. They will, for example, be able to seek out and destroy cancer cells, but also to stimulate hormone production, change your mood, and deliver medication right where you need it.

Smartwatches today can already detect early signs of illness including arrhythmias and infections, and they are even capable of pre-symptomatic detection of coronavirus disease (Mishra, 2020). Soon they will even be able to measure blood glucose levels and blood pressure. But it won't stop there. Over the next few years, I expect the next gadget to have will be the smart mirror that will help us with our health and wellbeing.

When more and more technological advances are made to keep us healthy, will I still have a job? Maybe not, and this is a scenario I must take into account. Another scenario is that demands will change. By that, I mean that the nature of the ailments that people come to me with will change. With new jobs, new challenges to our health and wellbeing will arise. For example, I can foresee that virtual or augmented reality will bring about more vestibular and neck problems. New forms of stress will also emerge when new technologies find their way into our lives. I have my finger on the pulse and keep questioning myself in order to be relevant as a healer.

The third scenario I apply is scanning the horizon for new opportunities that I can explore. For example, opportunities for my services in space tourism. Soon, private firms like Virgin Galactic and Blue Origin will fly you to the very edge of space and back. In the years to come, SpaceX will take you for a trip around the Earth or around the Moon and back. Oh yes, and the space hotel Voyager Station is planned to be operational in 2027.

If you're looking for an exciting new job, I would look to space or the off-world economy. The Space Foundation's The Space Report 2022 estimates that the space economy was worth $469 billion in 2021 (WEF, 2022). It is a growing market, expected to be worth trillions by 2040.

Not to sidetrack too much here, but the opportunity I see is that, unlike professional astronauts, private astronauts will not be selected for their physical or psychological prowess nor trained extensively for a mission of a lifetime. I can already predict a few health challenges that will need attending to where I can be of help. One is the physical strain when you go up or come down. Ever been on a rollercoaster ride with a lumbar disc out of place? Although going up into space and coming back down to Earth will be short, participants with little training will experience significant G-forces: this is described as like having a baby elephant sitting on you for a few minutes. On top of that, you have something called acceleration stress or the physiological changes that occur in the human body in motion as a result of a rapid increase of speed. But that is not the only form of stress that space tourists will experience. I can imagine it will be one of the most fearful, anxious, exhilarating adventures, with a zillion other emotions that will spike stress levels. There is no doubt in my mind that the whole experience will have more Life-change units (LCUs) in a couple of hours than most people get in a year or even several years. The more LCUs one experiences, the higher the likelihood of illness or an accident happening.

Life-change unit (LCU)

A unit of measurement on the Life Events Rating Scale, on which diverse life experiences are assigned numerical values in accordance with their stress-generating potential. For example, divorce and death of a spouse or significant other are ranked as high-stress generators on the scale, retirement falls about midscale, and moving to a new house and a change in sleeping habits are ranked progressively lower. Some research indicates that individuals with a high cumulative LCU score (i.e., a high potential-stress score) show more health changes than other participants.

(APA)

My Reaset Approach, which is based on osteopathic principles, is the answer to making sure that private astronauts are physically ready – and, when they are back, that their stress response is "reaset" (returned to ease) so their mind-blowing experiences won't blow their mind or lead to post-traumatic stress. If their stress response is not reaset, this would be a true disaster not only for them, their family and their work environment, but also for humanity.

Viewing the Earth from above is said to be a deeply moving and transformational experience. Frank White coined a term for this in 1987: the "overview effect". The overview effect is a cognitive shift in awareness reported by some astronauts during space flight, often while viewing the Earth from outer space. When back on Earth, astronauts show more pro-environmental attitudes and behaviours (Voski, 2020).

PS: Did you know that the photo "Earthrise" – the image of the Earth and some of the Moon's surface that was taken from the lunar orbit by astronaut William Anders on 24 December 1968 during the Apollo 8 mission – propelled the environmental movement and led to Earth Day being established? (Wetli, 2020) Just saying!

There have been 600 professional astronauts since Yuri Gagarin made his first space flight in 1961 (Clark, 2021). Hundreds of private astronauts worldwide are going to follow over the next five years and see the Earth from a cosmic perspective. So, hundreds experiencing the overview effect – hopefully with the same cognitive shift as professional astronauts.

Imagine the changes in attitude and behaviour that will evoke, and the potential impact this will have when they go back to work. These are CEOs, entrepreneurs, businesspeople, people fortunate enough to be able to fork out at least $200,000 for a few minutes in space.

This shift in awareness is exactly what we need. Seeing the Earth from space and seeing the Earth in space – this change of perspective – will be another small step for man, another giant leap for mankind. It will create a new kind of self-awareness and connectedness triggered through the stories these private astronauts will bring back and the changes they will implement. This cosmic perspective, I foresee, will create a global shift in our consciousness and make us grasp that we are here together and that the Earth is a home we need to protect. Protect today, not tomorrow, so that there will be a tomorrow.

All of this can happen in the blink of an eye, unless stress takes the upper hand with these astronauts. Again, professional astronauts are selected and trained for years to deal with the stresses of space flight. Private astronauts are not. Remember what stress does to your brain if it gets out of hand. Maybe not immediately, but over the course of a few months, it will become a problem and can lead to post-traumatic stress. Yes, you can get that from what is considered a positive experience too. When the stress response – from that once-in-a-lifetime experience – doesn't reaset by itself or with facilitation, it will lead to all kinds of physical health problems but also mood changes, cognitive and behavioural changes, social detachment, violence, etc. Not something you want to see in CEOs, leaders and entrepreneurs.

So I've made it part of my objective for 2030 to become an osteopath and body-centred stress coach for space tourists to make sure their experience is a once-in-a-lifetime transformative experience for the good of mankind.

A GREAT future for me is a future where we all flourish in the flow of evolution and thrive in a fast-changing world. How I want to contribute to that is by fulfilling my potential and evolving on purpose. That is my sacred mission.

The above is one of the scenarios for a resilient future for myself. Resilient in body, mind and spirit. A vision and approach to life created by linking many dots: my potential, personal and global needs, opportunities, and so much more. This is what motivates me and gives me energy. Keeping all these elements in mind helps me to monitor my situation and progress. It also keeps me on my toes "to adapt". I know I still have a lot to learn, and there will be challenges, but I have big hopes and dreams for my future and the future of humanity.

I believe it's time to move on, as we still have three more futures to discover that offer benefits for your health and wellbeing.

The Futures Effect

Chapter 4:
An Evolvable Future

We have a certain degree of control over the evolutionary process and can influence our own course. But the only way to accomplish this is by bringing into question the very way we think about consciousness and the universe; by questioning many fundamental assumptions underlying civilisation.

Edgar Mitchell

Connecting the dots

Evolution has progressed such that we must now assume a large measure of conscious control in our own evolutionary process, as human volition is in fact a fundamental characteristic of nature.

Edgar Mitchell

While in the process of writing this, I was flicking through the pages of my first book. As this is a follow-up, I thought it best to go back and refresh my memory of all that I had shared, and make notes of things I had remembered later that might be interesting to include in this one.

While reading, my attention was especially drawn to the various excerpts from my diaries that I had included. These excerpts are copied word-for-word or are an exact translation from my mother tongue, Dutch, and describe my precarious state of being in various situations. These excerpts were only added at the very end of the writing and publishing process. A decision I didn't take lightly. These were very personal experiences of my darkest days and experiences that I had never shared with anyone – not even my family. Making them public, of course, I wondered how, for example, my family would react, or my patients. How would the world react? Did I want people to know? In the end, I decided that it was better to open up. Tell it how it was or is.

Anyway, re-reading these excerpts, I'm drawn back into time, and I let the experiences unfold in front of my mind's eye. Like a scientist looking through a microscope, I observe. From a place above, I observe myself and my thoughts. My brain starts connecting the dots of different time periods and blends them into one intemporal sphere of thought that is now engraved in the always present, although so many other thoughts are lost.

I relive the desperation and anguish I felt. I had come to what seemed an end, had lost meaning and hope of ever feeling content, fulfilled and healthy. What was the point of living if there was no progress, no personal evolution, no feeling of advancing and becoming more complete with time? If life was just a continuous battle against the odds, with now and then a spark of joy, and then someday to die, I didn't want it.

I get goosebumps just thinking how far I had tumbled down the rabbit hole. If I hadn't opened up to Anne-Marie, the local pharmacist-become-friend (the full story you can read in *Futurize Yourself – Design your life on purpose*), about my problems, then who knows what would have happened. What would have happened if I didn't take the helping hand that was offered? What if I had been stubborn and kept on believing I didn't need help? My guess is I wouldn't be here now writing this story.

When you have dark thoughts, when you don't see a way out, please seek help. Find someone you can open up to. I know this is not easy; I've been there. But you are not alone. There are people out there who care.

If you don't want to talk about it to someone in your close environment, there are literally thousands of volunteers around the world that you can contact. People who feel called to help and support you, many of whom have been there. People who didn't see a way out but were helped themselves and now want to help others forward.

Check out:

www.suicidepreventionlifeline.org, www.rethink.org or an organisation near you and start that conversation. Here in Brussels, we have www.chsbelgium.org who are doing a great job.

> Or why not try a chatbot like Woebot that is designed to be used every day, for a few minutes at a time, and specifically targets conditions like depression and anxiety? The makers of Woebot have created this chatbot grounded in clinical research and powered by AI, so it is easy to talk to and so that it fits right into your life, whenever you want to chat.

If you know someone who is not feeling well or is having suicidal thoughts, please reach out to them. Don't ignore your gut feeling if you are concerned about someone. Make them feel they are not alone. Encourage them to talk about how they are feeling – and listen, don't judge. Yes, this is not easy, and you might feel completely out of your comfort zone. But saving a life is much more important than your discomfort. PS: If you feel uncomfortable talking to someone who has suicidal feelings, do a search on the internet and find information, e.g., on www.rethink.org on how to support someone.

In my practice, it does happen that people open up about their suicidal thoughts. Once I had a person walk in and say, "If you don't help me, I'll commit suicide when I return home." This was not an idle threat. I listened and treated her osteopathically to calm the autonomic nervous system and stress response. At one stage during the treatment, I was able to leave her resting for a moment. I found an excuse to walk out and called her partner, whose number I had, and told him the situation. I wanted to make sure that someone was there when she got home.

Each situation is different. I had a panicked mother call me in despair because her young son wanted to die. In a Q&A session after a presentation, I had a student ask what she could do for a friend who was having suicidal thoughts, but my perception was that she was actually the one having those thoughts. Whatever the situation, just listen, don't judge. I know from personal experience this is not the time you want to be judged. You want to be heard. For most, it takes a lot of courage to open up. Just be there for them, show you care about them.

Recently my book *Futurize Yourself* has been a trigger for some to open up to me. So, coming back to the doubts I had making public the experiences of my darkest days, I'm glad I did put them in.

In my case, my suicidal thoughts were caused by the fact that I couldn't see a way out of my predicament and couldn't see how I would ever have the good life I so much longed for. A life where I felt content, fulfilled, healthy, and could fulfil my aspirations. A life that made sense.

Now, more than 20 years later, I still want that more than anything. What I wanted then I want now, and I can't imagine that ever changing. For life as we know it, there has to be a purpose, a reason why life, we and all that is exist. If life had no purpose, we wouldn't exist and there would be no evolution as we know it. So, because we evolve – even though I personally didn't always feel I was, as a whole, we were – there must be a purpose. And what if, just maybe, our purpose is simply to evolve on purpose?

Now, once again connecting the dots in hindsight, it seems that the underlying messages in good and bad times have always been pointing towards the understanding that the purpose of life is to evolve on purpose. "What purpose are you giving your life, Tom?" Each personal crisis boiled down to this one message, but I didn't recognise or comprehend it at the time. I was living in unawareness. This wasn't on purpose (pun intended); I just didn't know, didn't have the tools or the wisdom needed to decipher the signs, the message.

A hint here, a nudge there, but I made no response. A bigger hint and nudge, and still no one was at home or listening. Like a vicious circle that became more pressing year after year, I was called to act but didn't know. I lived in ignorance, and it nearly killed me. Until someone pointed out the exit. The exit to a new (r)evolution, a futures (r)evolution, where I became the creator of the future that I could evolve into by my own volition.

The evolving sense of self

Don't be a victim of negative self-talk. Remember, you are listening.

Bob Proctor

> "Where was progress, the sense that we evolve? Weren't we – I mean wasn't I – supposed to advance somehow? Grow, get smarter, richer and more complete year upon year? I could see none of that. No, all I could see was that I was regressing, with life becoming more futile and hopeless by the minute."

Those were my thoughts upon awakening one morning in my cold, damp bedroom at the back of my shop. That was in 1999. Now it's 2022. What changed? What hasn't changed?

Remember Jeff Bezos's approach I mentioned earlier? "You can build a strategy on what won't change." So, what didn't change and will never change that I could build on?

Me…

What didn't change is what I am, and what I could build on is who I am. Or is it vice versa? I'm not a linguist, but my point is that I am still Tom, born in Antwerp (Belgium) one early September morning in 1970, a male human, 180 cm tall and medium build. Who I am – or, better, have become and evolved into – is a proactive human being who consciously chooses to create a good life and GREAT future for himself and others rather than waiting for the proverbial great-life bus that never comes.

Choosing and walking the path I had chosen wasn't an easy process, and I can't claim I did it knowingly at first. Yes, I had – with help – defined a future that I imagined would, if realised, make more sense and result in being more fulfilled. But it wasn't as if I then organised a board meeting and started to brainstorm how to make the future I had designed on purpose a reality. Far from it!

My first steps towards my preferred future happened because, some time after I had written down my vision of becoming a therapist who had developed his own approach and so on, I was invited to an information evening about kinesiology. As soon as I saw what kinesiology was, I knew that this was something for me. I can't explain it. I felt this technique ticked many of the boxes that would lead me to realise my future as a therapist. It was like a moment of clarity in which my future me was linked with my present me, and my future me was telling me: "That's for you, start there, go, go, go, Tom."

I listened to my future me and enrolled on the first course available. For me, taking my first steps learning kinesiology felt like coming home. Rarely had I done anything new that had given me that sensation of being where I was meant to be and doing what I was designed to do. It must have been written all over my face, as this feeling hadn't gone unnoticed by the instructor. So, during one of the exercises, she asked me if I had done this before or had any prior experience. Nope, never; it was my first time, and I loved it. After hearing this, she told me: "If you like this, I'm sure you'll like…," and gave me a list of courses I could take not so far away – and off I went.

I still had my deli at the time, and because that wasn't bringing in enough money, I was also doing other work. At first, I went to work in a local bistro as a waiter, then at a catering firm. This was so I could pay for these courses that didn't come cheap, but working extra hours was a small price to pay for the joy these courses gave me.

This joy didn't only come from the content of the courses, but also because I was meeting people just like me. I always had been the odd one out wherever I had been and whatever I'd done. However, at these courses, I found people who came from far and wide who were just like me – a bit different, but eager to learn and become the best version of themselves. Straight away there was this deeper connection, and with some, I felt, even though it was the first time, that I had known them all my life. For it was like finally finding my family, my soul family.

Those first steps exposing me to what I had envisaged were such a revelation that I started to believe that I actually could change and have the future I had envisaged.

Next steps

Where focus goes, energy flows. And where energy flows, whatever you're focusing on grows. In other words, your life is controlled by what you focus on. That's why you need to focus on where you want to go, not on what you fear. When you next find yourself in a state of uncertainty, resist your fear. Shift your focus toward where you want to go and your actions will take you in that direction.

Tony Robbins

As mentioned before, in the beginning I wasn't really aware that I was actively creating my future. I just cruised forward on the river of life – with the difference that I had a direction. A focal point I wanted to get to, and through which I was always able to weigh up the opportunities that came my way. It was only after some years that I became more aware that it was the future that was pushing and pulling me forward. With that awareness came also the intentional use of it. Today, I would even say it is an integrated, dynamic and ever-evolving (problem-solving – stress management) tool that I not only use for long-term but also medium and short-term changes and challenges. It has become part of me.

> Recently I read a very interesting research article by Futures & Trends Researcher Akash Das (IMCI, 2022) on the value and role of indigenous and tribal knowledge in planetary and climate foresight. It mentions that for many indigenous people/tribes: "… anticipatory decision making, is interwoven in their ways of living, cultivated as an integral and intrinsic tool for their survival, safety & well-being, since centuries."

By "integrated" I mean that I always have one eye on my North Star, my preferred future. The preferred future which all my decisions, choices and actions are aligned with to help me move forward.

For example, after I had closed my deli, I decided never to work with any kind of product again that I wouldn't have with me on a nudist beach. I suppose that last part needs some explanation. In my deli, where I was selling various hams and cheeses, I had to throw away a lot that was going to spoil because I didn't have sufficient turnaround. It broke my heart, as I was raised not to throw food away. Also, I had been around the world and seen poverty in many places, including India, and had been to the shantytowns and slums of Soweto and Khayelitsha in South Africa. Seeing poverty left a big impression.

So when I closed the doors of the deli for the last time, I vowed to never work with any kind of product again. Also, my potential "traveller" that I've come to associate with the need of freedom of movement excluded the use of a product. Because part of what the future I wanted and needed was to be so free that I could do my job anytime, anyplace, anywhere.

That is the case today. You can pick me up right here and now, put me on a plane or a spaceship, and I can do what I do. I can treat people, I can teach people, I can mentor people. I can do everything I do in my practice. If the Sun unleashed a coronal mass ejection – which is an immense cloud of magnetised particles – in Earth's direction and destroyed our entire electronic infrastructure, I can still do what I do today and every day.

At first, this – what some might call an obsession – was a reaction against waste; so it is, but later I recognised it as part of my innate need for liberty and independence. This need is also why I don't want a cat or a dog, as these would tie me down.

"Nudist beach" as a metaphor: yes, I know my brain works in mysterious ways, but this has made many laugh and has helped me make choices. Choices, for example, about which courses to follow. Was the proposed course leading to a technique I could do on my nudist beach or not? That became my standard reflection. When I chose osteopathy over acupuncture, it was also because there weren't any needles on a nudist beach, so that choice was eliminated.

I also used and still use this metaphor when, for example, the phone rings and somebody tries to convince me to sell this or that in my practice. I just say no. When they ask why not, I give them my nudist beach metaphor, and I have never had someone persisting after that. It has also helped me to say "No" at times without being rude or feeling guilty about it.

There are so many options, possibilities and opportunities open to us. How do you know what to choose when you don't know what you want? How do you stay focused when you don't know where you are going? Having a narrative for your future, a symbolic framework that you build your life around, helps you to evolve on purpose.

Living more intentionally and with focus also leads you from being a passenger of life to being the driver. I had to learn the hard way that waiting for the world to come to me was not how life worked. Sitting on the sidelines waiting was what got me into trouble. As a kid, I didn't know any better, and it was a behaviour that was very difficult to shake off.

Repeating patterns

Do not let the shadows of your past darken the doorstep of your future.

Anonymous

Writing this down reminds me of a moment with my dad just before the publication of *Futurize Yourself – Design your life on purpose*. Dad and I were on our way to see Herman van Veen, a famous Dutch singer, writer and artist.

My dad who has several sculptures in the Herman van Veen Arts Center (Soest, NL) had been personally invited by Herman as a guest of honour, and I could come along. We were chauffeured there and so had time to talk.

My book includes several passages which refer to mostly difficult moments with my parents that still influence me today. It also mentions my suicidal thoughts, challenges and periods of self-mutilation, which I had never spoken to them about. The book was their first introduction to these difficult events. I thought this drive would maybe be an opportunity for my dad to say something about what he had read. But no, the only reference he made to it was that it wasn't always easy to read. That was it. Dad is a man of few words.

The next day at the breakfast table, I asked him something I had been wondering about. No, I didn't ask what he had been thinking when he first read about my various struggles. If he wasn't going to say anything about it, I wasn't going to ask. It was not important. What I did ask was how he saw me as a kid. I said to him: "From my book, you know how I saw you. What I'd like to know is how you saw me." I don't think he saw that one coming, but our relationship is such that I can say things like that. I feel more at ease to do so now, and I know that, if I don't ask, I won't ever know the answer.

My dad will never divulge something of his own accord, but he is always happy when people ask him questions. He's also always eager to help, but you have to ask. I wish I had known that when I was a kid. But I'm running ahead here.

So, me over breakfast: "Dad, you've read my book and you know now how I saw you, but how did you see me?"

He pondered on that for a while, and in typical-of-my-dad fashion, his answer was very short – but he didn't need to say anything more. Dad said: "When parents have children, what often happens is that they forget about themselves. Everything starts to revolve around the child. I was not like that. When you wanted to do something with me, that was OK, and if you didn't, that was OK too." That was it. That was all the explanation I received.

But I understood. I wanted my dad to come to me, and my dad functioned on the main premise that I had to come to him.

I'm telling a lie here. He also said I wasn't a kid that was interested in handiwork. In French they call it a bricoleur, a handyman. When he was a kid, he had learned to work wood, sculpt and paint from his dad. I hadn't shown any interest in that, so he didn't teach me.

I didn't agree with his analyses, because when I stayed with my grandparents, I was always with my grandad in the cellar creating things. The difference was that my grandad asked me, or rather told me. "Come on, Tom, let's go and create… or do…" Grandad also took me to the market, museums and we did plenty of activities together. Probably also because Grandad, "den Bompa", had time. Dad, by his own account, didn't do that. Dad also didn't have time. He worked full-time and built our house, etc. Anyway, this isn't the point. The point is that Grandad initiated the action. With Dad, it was me who had to initiate the action. "When you wanted to do something with me…" It's the direction of the phrase that for me was illuminating.

But my main behavioural characteristic was "sitting on the sidelines" waiting for the world to come to me. Dad was waiting for me and I for him, and we didn't get anywhere, or at least we weren't understanding each other, until much later.

Now, what do you know?! I just had an "Aha!" moment. Why did I wait for the world to come to me? My world was my grandad. In my early years, he was my role model, because I spent more time with my grandparents than I did at home – or, if not more, at least a lot. All my memories of my early years are never at the parental home but always at my grandparents' home. I had learned from a young age that it was the norm that the world came to me.

Maybe I'm over-intellectualising it, but for me this revelation is meaningful. Also, I'm not judging here. I'm just observing, and as behaviour is often set in the first few years of life, maybe my behaviour of sitting and waiting for the world to come to me was born there, or at least seeded.

A behaviour that was challenged when what I was handed – "the opportunity of opening my own deli" – turned out to be a prison from which I could see no escape. That behaviour nearly killed me, and challenging it was a hard nut to crack. I'm not even sure that I master it fully today, but I'm getting better at it.

Let's come back to other processes that were helping me forward, like fishing.

Catching opportunities

Excuses will always be there for you. Opportunity won't.

Anonymous

By now you should know that my brain works in mysterious ways and that at times, to share a story or insight, I go off the beaten track to shed some light on the experience. So here is another one of these weird-and-wonderful quirky metaphors which might at first make you frown a bit, and it's about fishing.

I'm not a fisherman myself, but when I walk around the pond in the park near our home, I often see how the hobby fishermen have not only one line out but several, which I can only imagine is to increase their opportunities or chances to catch a fish.

In much the same way, but without the fishing line, plans or paths can be explored and projects started to land opportunities. For example, writing this book has the primary objective of helping you to adopt and reap the benefits of a futures mindset, but it is also meant as a business card for landing opportunities to speak. Speaking and giving workshops is something I'd like to do more in the years to come.

However, a book doesn't get written by itself. I know it sounds silly: of course not, Tom! But how many people want to write a book that never materialises because they never put pen to paper, so to speak? How many people say: "Oh, you're so lucky! I wish I…" – but, when told how to invite luck or boost their luck, they always have an excuse not to follow up on it. This is not a reproach. Everyone has their own learning curve. A good quote to remember is: "Destiny is no matter of chance. It is a matter of choice. It is not a thing to be waited for, it is a thing to be achieved" (William Jennings Bryan).

Yes, I know it sounds obvious, but I had to find this out the hard way. I was a bit naive when I was younger and thought that the world of opportunities would drop itself at my feet. But look where that got me. As mentioned before, I was a teeny-weeny bit conditioned by circumstances. Once I understood that I had to be more proactive and could create opportunities and make decisions that worked for me, that was the next step in my process of evolving on purpose.

So I not only aligned my decisions, choices and actions with my preferred future in mind; I also made sure I paved my way forward intentionally. I think another illustration is in order here.

Imagine you have a dream and you keep it all to yourself. You tell no one, not even your best friend. Only your mirror knows it, because you've been repeating your dream to it every morning and evening for the past 10 years: "Mirror, mirror on the wall, I wish for…"

Believe me when I say that talking about your dream to someone works much better than telling it to your mirror to make it come true. It helps, but, I think, only if others with whom you share it see it in you or believe in you and your dream. Believe that you have it in you, that it is actionable. But more about "actionable" later. For now, believe me that, if your dream is to be a prince and you were not born into a royal family, they will probably laugh and say: "You can't be serious!" or "You can always try for the Carnival Prince." OK, don't get me wrong: it does happen. A personal trainer did become Prince Daniel, Duke of Västergötland in Sweden. But I think you know what I'm getting at.

Many people keep their dreams to themselves, are afraid to put themselves forward, and I get that. Fear of being ridiculed or criticised or having one's dream stolen. I know what that fear feels like – I've been there. However, when your dream is sincere, comes from within and serves your purpose, and when you ask people to help you, I see that, more often than not, it leads to a positive response. It might take time.

When I shared my dream of becoming an osteopath with an osteopath, I got a message back from him two months later that a friend of his was setting up a school. Six years later (2007), I was a certified osteopath. Then (as mentioned before) at an osteopathy conference in Berlin, I had a conversation with German colleagues about the impossible dream of obtaining the Diploma of Osteopathy. I was denied this in Belgium after I had received my certification. This meant that my patients were not reimbursed by social security. So he said, "Why don't you enrol on the Bachelor and Masters in Osteopathy course at the Osteopathie Schule Deutschland?" Er, what? There is a BSc and MSc course? Two years later I had my BSc and all that was needed to get my D.O. and recognition in Belgium. Four years later I also had my MSc. All that because I spoke up about my impossible dream.

Having a website, being on podcasts, creating TEDxVilvoorde on the topic of "What, the Future?!" and the many articles I've written – all this is not only because I like doing these things or because I feel the need to inform people better. Yes, they are part of expressing my purpose to empower people to flourish in the flow of evolution and thrive in a fast-changing world, but they are also to create opportunities for me to grow and evolve. Sometimes it takes years before I catch a fish – I mean, land an opportunity.

For example, earlier this year, I saw on LinkedIn that someone had translated "Stress: the health epidemic of the 21st century" into Turkish. An article I wrote four years ago. I thanked them for it. I could have disputed whether this was legal or not because they hadn't asked me – which I must admit was my first reaction. In principle, republishing an article without prior permission is not done. OK, they did link and credited me, and I didn't see any harm done, so I wrote and thanked them without comment. This led to a conversation and an invitation to be a keynote speaker at their Future of Work conference. A conference I hadn't heard of – but with the main topic "Unlocking human potential in these fast-changing times" and more than 2,000 international attendees, I was very interested, to say the least.

If I hadn't written that article, they might have never heard about me. Nor would I have had other opportunities that have manifested which are directly linked to the keynote address I gave.

Again, I write articles and go on podcasts to empower others to flourish and thrive in these fast-changing times – that is my first ambition. But at the back of my mind, there is always an intention and hope that they might lead to other opportunities to increase the realisation of my first ambition.

I give these examples to make you, the reader, think about – yes, I know, I'm going to say it again: "What the future do you want?" More specifically, how to make what you want happen. I've said it before: I was very naive. I was waiting for the world to fall at my feet. No, I wasn't arrogant – far from it – but just unworldly. Although I had travelled around the world, I just didn't really grasp or understand the ways of the world. A trait that I've heard entrepreneurs and businesspeople complain about as regards to some younger employees.

When I realised that the world wasn't revolving around me and that change would not come if I waited for some other person or some other time, I was ready to move on. I was ready to build and work for the future I longed for.

Making decisions that work for you

Not all dreams are meant to come true, but when undertaken, to be revealing.

Tom Meyers

I've been told that one of my traits is to "re-search for the answer". I do what? That was the first thought going through my mind when I heard it. However, once the words sank in, I had to give Fredrik Haren – The Creativity Explorer – credit for figuring me out so well after a very short conversation on establishing my inner theme.

Re-searching for the answer – yes, that is something I do. I seem, indeed, to have an inquisitive mind that has a tendency to wonder, and to question some set ideas and philosophies of life we have adopted. That wondering and questioning – that is what Fredrik meant.

For example, in my previous book I question the quote, "If you can imagine it, you can achieve it. If you can dream it, you can become it." Another quote I have questioned in an article is: "Life is like a box of chocolates. You never know what you're gonna get." Really? … you NEVER know what you are going to get?

I don't question everything all the time (rest assured!), but when I do it's like a flashbulb going off in my head after I've heard, read or even said something myself that suddenly says: "Hang on a minute. That feels off." For example, the statement: "Life can only be understood backwards but must be lived forwards." It's a quote from Søren Kierkegaard that I used in my previous book. It seemed fitting at the time of writing to illustrate how I got to where I had been when my life crisis hit me.

While writing this chapter, though, I thought about that Kierkegaard quote again, and (yes, you can hear me coming) it suddenly felt incomplete, discordant, somehow off, and I couldn't let it go. So I started searching the internet to get some background on the quote, and it turns out that the quote is but a paraphrased quotation of what Kierkegaard wrote. So here is the complete paragraph translated from Danish: "It is quite true what philosophy says, that life must be understood backwards. But then one forgets the other principle, that it must be lived forward. Which principle, the more one thinks it through, ends exactly with temporal life never being able to be properly understood, precisely because I can at no instant find complete rest to adopt the position: backward" (Kirmmse, 2008).

What do you think? I don't consider myself knowledgeable about philosophy, but for me the full phrase tells a slightly different story – and, reading some blogs on the topic, it seems that I'm not the only one who thinks this.

First of all, Kierkegaard said: "life **must** be understood backwards..." and not "life **can only** be understood backwards..." There is big difference between "must" and "can only". "Can only" to me means there is no other way, while "must", on the other hand, isn't that determined.

When I spoke about my thoughts to one of my dear futures thinking allies and the founder of Silicon Humanism, Sylvia Gallusser, she responded: "'must' is interesting on many levels: is it a 'must' in the sense of requirement in the thought process, or in the sense of moral obligation to live a better life, or is it closer to a 'should' as an advice or a recommendation, or is it a probability (people tend to...), etc.?"

So what did Kierkegaard mean?

A sense of requirement, obligation, advice or something else, however you choose to interpret "life must be understood backwards". It doesn't say it is the only way. Yes, we should consider the past, look backwards. We must learn from our experiences, so to speak, to understand where we are, but it isn't the "only" timeframe to consider.

When we look more closely at the words and the context of what Kierkegaard said, we also need to take into account that, for him, temporal life can't be understood properly. This is because there is no moment where you can adopt the position: backward. By this, he apparently meant that there is neither present nor past nor future, as life is ongoing. For me, that again doesn't say per se that "life **can only** be understood backwards".

"Life **must** be understood backwards..." How I understand that is that we should contemplate our past, to better figure out how we got here today in this moment, but as life is ongoing, we also have to realise that as soon as you think it, that moment is already in the past. This makes it really difficult to understand life to the full.

But "life must be lived forward," as Kierkegaard states. This is what shouldn't be forgotten. He draws our attention to this. Yes, we may not be able to understand life to the full, but what we do know is that it must be lived forward. Something I've been trying to draw your attention to every time I mention that every decision and choice you make, and every action you take, influences y'our future.

Are you still with me? I know it is a winding road that I'm paving for you while writing this, but I know where I'm going, so please stay with me for a while longer.

Chapter 4: An Evolvable Future

Before I go on contemplating this, I'd like to mention another more recent quote that I have found while digging deeper into Kierkegaard's paraphrased quote. That quote is from the late Steve Jobs (one of the founders of Apple) who said in his 2005 commencement address at Stanford University: "You can't connect the dots looking forward; you can only connect them looking backwards. So you have to trust that the dots will somehow connect in your future. You have to trust in something – your gut, destiny, life, karma, whatever. This approach has never let me down, and it has made all the difference in my life."

I wonder if Steve Jobs was a chess player? Chess players see multiple moves ahead. In other words, they see and connect the dots forward. They see in their mind a few moves ahead, with different scenarios for how the opposing player might react and plans to counteract. Looks to me a lot like connecting dots forward.

Learning from our past is essential and, yes, we – including me – often connect the dots in hindsight. This book and my previous one are full of insights, dots and learnings. Life must be lived forward, that is evident, and life only exists to us in the ongoing present, I get that – but is it truly so that life "can only" be understood, or that we can only connect the dots, backwards? As you have read, I contest that.

Yes, we must look backwards to understand where we are, but the past is not the only timeframe influencing our present. The future might not exist, but, like a chess player, we can imagine future scenarios and have them influence our decisions, choices and actions – and therefore our ongoing present. We can learn from thinking what we want and don't want the future to be. We can backcast, meaning we can define our desirable future and then work backwards and identify dots, which are ideas or steps that can connect that specified future to the present, to then influence our decisions, choices and actions. What has got me here is the past but, for more than 20 years now, that past has been guided and influenced by the future I wanted and designed on purpose.

By the way – and thank you for pointing this out to me, Sylvia – I do not contest that not everything can be rationalised. Sometimes you have to trust your gut, destiny, life, karma, whatever. Like for Steve Jobs, this approach has often made the difference in my life too.

My point in waffling on about this is: don't let yourself be limited by the past. Adopt a futures mindset where you learn and understand your ongoing reality by learning from the past but also from the possibilities of y'our future and, by doing so, better understand your present. This futures mindset will help you to evolve on purpose. The benefits are that you will be much better able to cope and navigate not only many of the current changes and challenges but also future ones.

I'd like to back this up with the following: "Energy flows where attention goes." To adopt a futures-included mindset, your intention matters. Intent encourages y'our subconscious mind to bring forth a desired goal, as well as the most optimal future (Hallbom, 2012). With intention, the subconscious mind can link with your conscious mind, and you'll be able to see, hear and understand the things that will help you get to what you want or what you're intending. You'll be able to connect the dots forward. I really want you to spend some time thinking about this. Disagree if you want, but please think about it. Think about what the future you want, and when you have a clear image of the future you want, how will you get what you want or intend? That will depend on what you do today – your decisions, choices, actions and your thoughts.

I know it might be a bit of a challenge getting to grips with this. To help you, do some research yourself on Kierkegaard's quote and expand your search to the Reticular Activating System (RAS). The what…? The RAS is the part of your brain right above the brainstem which is responsible for connecting the subconscious part of your brain with the conscious part. It's super interesting in connection with what we've just been discussing.

What is important now is that with intent (to have a course of action) and intention (the action of intending), the future becomes far less mysterious, and you not only start to live forward but start to understand more and more about life, and connect dots going forward. Futurizing yourself to create a GREAT future where you evolve on purpose means using and, by default, developing this innate potential you have. It means letting your intention create into reality what the future you want.

Before I started to evolve on purpose, I needed to revisit my past. Revisit it and change some of the narrative. I had a deformed image of my past, and if I had continued believing I was good for nothing then I wouldn't be an osteopath, author or wellbeing futurist today. But just revisiting my past and changing my narrative would have made no difference if I hadn't adopted a futures-included mindset. It is the future that pulled me forward. Past and future combined help me to understand life better – and, step by step over the years, have helped me to be and feel content, fulfilled and healthy, and to have what I so much longed for.

Addendum

Let me quickly come back to you as regards Kierkegaard's words. I wanted to be one hundred per cent sure that the translation that I had found on the internet and also put through Google Translate was correct. So I contacted Marianne, a dear Danish friend, and asked her.

By the way, the original words are: "Det er ganske sandt, hvad Philosophien siger, at Livet maa forstaaes baglaends. Men derover glemmer man den anden Saetning, at det maa leves forlaends. Hvilken Saetning, jo meer den gjennemtaenkes, netop ender med, at Livet i Timeligheden aldrig ret bliver forstaaeligt, netop fordi jeg intet Øieblik kan faae fuldelig Ro til at indtage Stillingen: baglaends."

"Livet maa forstaaes baglaends" does indeed translate to "life must be understood backwards." A thumbs-up for my feeling that something was off. Why do I suddenly have to think of Luke Skywalker and Yoda…? LOL.

Marianne also pointed out, and for some reason I hadn't spotted it, that in Kierkegaard's text he uses "Livet maa forstaaes baglaends" and "det maa leves forlaends." So twice "maa" which means "must", so why someone decided to translate his first "maa" as "can only" is a mystery to me. But something important got lost in translation, if you ask me.

As you see y'our future, so you act. As you act, ...

We are responsible for what we are, and whatever we wish ourselves to be, we have the power to make ourselves. If what we are now has been the result of our own past actions, it certainly follows that whatever we wish to be in the future can be produced by our present actions; so we have to know how to act.

Swami Vivekananda

I would like you to believe me when I say that it is a small step to take, but a giant leap in your evolution, to futurize yourself. But the best thing is to experience it yourself. I took that one step more than 20 years ago when I was depressed and suicidal. It worked out for me.

Now, knowing why it worked for me, I see it as my sacred duty to pass on my experiences and ideas to make it work for you. Nothing would make me happier than to hear that it helped you evolve, flourish and thrive and have a GREAT future.

The future doesn't just happen. Every decision and choice you make or do not make, and every action you take or do not take, influences the outcome of y'our future. I can't repeat this enough. I can't repeat enough the importance of this fact. I've gone through a part of my life in ignorance of this, but – oh my! – has it made a positive impact on my life since I learned it and started to live life forward consciously, on purpose!

I must admit that, in sharing this, I must put aside many apprehensions I have that my words might seem less of an encouragement than they are intended to be. I'm not here to lecture you or come over as a guru. I'm here to inform, make you think, and foremost to help you make up your own mind. So always keep an open mind. Don't copy-paste me (or anyone, for that matter) without reflection.

Futurizing yourself and evolving on purpose will have you spending time doing some serious introspection, outrospection and futures inspection, i.e., prospection.

> **Outrospection** is a term coined by Australian philosopher and author of *The Good Ancestor*, Roman Krznaric (2021) and defined as: "A method in which you get to know yourself by developing relationships and empathic thinking with others."

The benefits of this time well spent are enriching and rewarding for the rest of your life. Yes, it will also challenge you over and over again, as you will have to put into question your own beliefs, biases, assumptions, experiences and more.

Does it sound like a lot of work? Well, it is, but y'our quality of life depends on it. Life just ain't a walk in the park – and leaving it up to chance has become a deadly game.

The good thing is that our behaviour precedes the future, and our behaviour is preceded by our thoughts and images of the future, which in turn are preceded by our feelings. So don't stress. Breathe…

It's easier than you think, and it starts with accepting that the future cannot be known – that uncertainty reigns – and that, instead of struggling against it, you can embrace it. "Life is so much easier than you think it is, and as you come to understand the way life works, and the power you have inside you, you will experience the magic of life in its fullness" (Rhonda Byrne).

You already can adapt to short and medium-term changes. Look how quickly we adapted and evolved to a new normal in response to the COVID-19 pandemic. We could have done better if we had been more proactive, but let it be the lesson we had to learn. The lesson we now need to remember and integrate to pull us/you forward.

Yes, it will require your time and attention acquiring a futures mindset – but, in all honesty, if you think about it, what doesn't? Always keep in mind that the time you spend futurizing yourself is to enable you to have and live what the future you want. If you want to build a GREAT future where you feel content, fulfilled and healthy, and flourish and thrive in this fast-changing world, then you have no choice but to work at it. There is no alternative.

We all know by now that we are experiencing huge challenges and that more challenges await us. We are, so to speak, at the fork in the road where we will need to make a choice.

> Humanity has entered a critical moment in its history. The coming decade is a time of great historical significance, and the decisions humanity collectively makes in the next 10 years may well determine whether our future is bright and prosperous, or whether it leads to misery and perhaps even our eventual demise as a species.
>
> From the Fork in the Road Project: The Manifesto (2021)

If we want to tackle the current challenges and those ahead, we need to stop putting our heads in the sand and ignoring our future or refusing to think about it; otherwise, the consequences will be devastating.

Putting it off is putting your life, and that of your family and humanity as a whole, in the balance. In essence, the empowering message of futurizing yourself is defined by this quote: "As you see y'our future, so you act. As you act, so you and y'our world become." A quote I adapted from Barbara Marx Hubbard: "As you see the future, so you act, and as you act so you become!"

By now, I hope you have thought about y'our future. Where you are going, what you want, but also where we are going together as one. We are, after all, speeding through space together on Spaceship Earth. PS: Did you know that the Earth orbits the Sun at 107,226 km/h and covers about 2.6 million km a day, while the Sun and the solar system are moving at 720,000 km/h in the Milky Way? We are in the same boat, so to speak, together.

I know research is part of my potential – and that means, I suppose, that questioning things comes rather naturally to me now, but I had to learn it. Learn by doing once it was pointed out to me that I could.

I see around me, hear and read in the media that we don't question things any more. Take the spreading of fake news, for example: how many people literally copy-paste information without giving it the slightest scrutiny? Been there, done that – but I hope to avoid it now by being a bit more aware, I suppose you could say.

Anyway, I don't want to be a moralist, but I know that questioning, especially questioning myself, enriched me. I would even say it saved me, and through it, I was able to give my life a direction, meaning and purpose.

How did I get here? Where am I going? What can I do better? What's my potential? What do I need in order to feel whole inside? These questions helped me, still do, and I hope they can help you to evolve on purpose. This is in combination with trusting and following your gut feelings. Some things you just can't know, and that is OK too. Let's use all our potential to evolve on purpose and grow into the person we were born to be.

Can we evolve on purpose?

Evolve or dissolve... It's your decision.

Larry Price

Give or take a little, but lasting evolutionary change takes about one million years. Biological evolution is a constant and sometimes rapid process. However, the changes that hit and stick tend to take a long time (Uyeda et al., 2011).

On the other hand, societal, cultural and technological changes are evolving fast and continue to evolve exponentially. But while we possess a great capacity for change, our ability to manage change is still very limited (Wilson et al., 2014).

> The human mind can be described as "a set of information-processing machines that were designed by natural selection to solve adaptive problems faced by our hunter-gatherer ancestors." Because our modern skull houses a Stone-Age mind, "The key to understanding how the modern mind works is to realise that its circuits were not designed to solve the day-to-day problems of a modern American – they were designed to solve the day-to-day problems of our hunter-gatherer ancestors."
>
> (Wilson et al., 2014)

The question is: how will we bridge the gap? The fact that you experience more stress today has much to do with this conflict of our slow biological evolution in a fast-changing environment which we have created. When you don't manage this conflict or navigate it, dis-ease – i.e., stress – will set in. Chronic dis-ease/stress will lead to distress and illness. Put simply, it is a question of demands outweighing your resources. Just like the Earth, your resources are limited and take time to restore when used. So, the more demands there are on you without time to recuperate and regenerate – well, problems are inevitable.

> In parentheses: **The Ecological Footprint** (EF) is a measure of human demand on natural capital (i.e., the quantity of nature it takes to support people or an economy), and a Life Change Unit (LCU) is the unit of measurement on the Life Events Rating Scale, on which different life experiences are assigned numerical values in accordance with their stress-generating potential. I wonder if you can make the following comparison: the Ecological Footprint (EF) is for the Earth what Life Change Units (LCU) are for us human beings. What do you think?

Much has changed since our forebears roamed the plains, but the fact is that, just as there is no Earth II, there is no replacement for your body. This is it! Just saying…

We can't wait a million years to catch up with the exponential changes of the digital age we have created. A digital age that will bring along more change and further increase the demands on us. So what now?

We need to engage in purposeful evolution. In other words, evolve on purpose and mind the future we want to evolve into.

"We are agents in the ongoing evolution of evolution, and what constitutes evolution as it moves forward in time is up to us."

These are the words of futurist and author Thomas Lombardo. I know I've mentioned his book *Future Consciousness: The Path to Purposeful Evolution* several times already, but it is well worth your attention if you are interested in a more scientifically informed and psychologically holistic approach to understanding how our unique conscious minds reflect and amplify nature's vast evolutionary process.

We need to start thinking about our future, the future we want. A future where we manage the changes ahead of time to flourish and thrive as individuals and as a whole. We have the potential to change ourself and our environment with purpose to suit a purpose. That purpose can be influencing our own evolution. Yes, we can do that. It is truly up to you how we evolve and where we are going, now that you are conscious of it.

Side note:

I'd like to point out that the evolving on purpose that I'm talking about doesn't involve integrating or becoming technology. As soon as you start on that path, you are more likely to lose your agency – especially when it involves integrating some form of artificial intelligence that thinks and acts for you.

Some may think that this is the next evolution of humankind. It is a path, but it seems to me to be a dead-end road.

My simplistic brain really has a problem with this type of evolution, because brain implantations or that optimised robot arm, just like plastic surgery results for that matter, do not get passed on to your offspring.

How can we call that evolution? Tamper with the brain and you temper with life and free will. That is not even taking into account that any electronic device is hackable. Just imagine that you are subjected to someone else's will because he hacked your neurolink, robotic arm or pacemaker!

So, if you ask me, integrating technology into your body makes you very vulnerable, and you risk becoming a slave. But maybe we are already digital slaves dancing to the tunes of a few.

We have evolved over millions of years to have a magnificent brain and body with unfathomable potential. When given a purpose, a direction, our intention and attention to it will determine whether or not we develop the potential that is within us.

But do you have the courage to make it a priority?

Avoid distractions and stay focused

Distract from distraction – your future self will thank you more quickly.

Tom Meyers

I was going to write a bit more about my thoughts on transhumanism and the side effects of brain implants on our evolution as individuals and as a species. However, trying to put my thoughts down in writing, I noticed that I was struggling. Suddenly my writing became haggard, and the more I struggled, the more I felt disconnected, moody and tired.

A week went by, then two, of writing, rewriting and just not finding the flow. The more it went on like this, the more I became frustrated. What was happening? This was an interesting, even fascinating topic. Tampering with the brain and the make-up of our body was tampering with life and our evolution and thus must be considered if we want a GREAT future. My personal belief is that integrating technology can't be the answer to our evolution. I needed to write about this, but when I did, it was like wading through the mud, and with every step I took, I was struggling more, not getting any closer to my goal. I couldn't make head or tail of it, so it was time for a timeout. A moment to step back, take an overview and see where I was going with this with reference to where I wanted to go. Was this resistance I was feeling because I was being distracted, taking me away from my objective? Were the reflections I had been trying to summarise on the adverse health effects and our evolution a step too far for this book, for me? Or was this resistance because I needed to learn something and grow?

I decided it was the first – a distraction and deviation from the essence. The reflections were good. We must question whether the integration of technology is really what it is made out to be. We must think, besides the side effects on our own health and wellbeing, whether, for example, there might not be transgenerational side effects too. Our life and that of future generations depend on it.

Anyway, I removed all I had written from my ongoing document and saved it in another for later. Although it's important, I wasn't ready for this discussion, and it was too far outside my field of expertise.

It's a bit frustrating, but one has to recognise one's limits – and I'm glad I did realise this because, as if by magic, in the days that followed, the oppression I felt within left me. My head became clearer, and slowly I started to feel connected again.

I could have kept this experience to myself, but I decided it was better to write about it while it was happening. It is a perfect example of how I've experienced the futures effect over the past 20 years and realised the future I had designed on purpose. It is these experiences (which can seem insignificant for others) that have made the difference for me. This is how I embraced my evolutionary future. This is how I left randomness behind and started to live intentionally, creating the future I wanted.

The Futures Effect

Embracing y'our evolvable future

You must let go of your past and embrace your future and figure out what path you're going to go down.

George Lucas

Back to our evolvable future. You know by now that I can ask some seemingly straightforward questions which, on second thoughts, aren't so straightforward after all. So here is another one: "How do you know that you are evolving?"

I consider that you, just like all human beings, have an innate desire to evolve, to become better somehow. Consciously seek to grow into a better version of themselves. Don't you? But how do you measure that? How do you – yes, you – measure how you are evolving over time?

Can you imagine not evolving? Meaning staying the same year after year. I can't imagine it. I think it is human nature that you want to improve yourself, to grow. We want to rise above what we were before.

You may think, again, "Whatever, Tom" – but, to me, being aware of my evolution and being able to measure it are key to doing better and making decisions that matter. Decisions that get me in the direction of what I want.

When I reflect on how I started to be more aware of my evolution, and to see the evidence that I was growing into the person I was born to be, I realise that I only became conscious of it once I had found my potential (therapist, communicator, teacher, researcher and explorer). Found my potential and given myself a life-long purpose that I could and wanted to pursue.

So it was only once I had my statement: "I'm a therapist with my own private practice and am invited to give presentations and workshops around the world relating to a new health approach I've developed, researched and written a book about" that I was able to make informed decisions and choices and take informed actions that mattered – and was also able to evaluate my progress.

I needed this. I needed a framework which I could use in order to deal with the myriad challenges I was faced with and create a more meaningful life – a life where I could evolve.

My random life from before had worn me thin and distracted to the point of distraction. Although the bohemian lifestyle had been a blessing in disguise, because, as a late bloomer, I needed time to grow up. However, when playtime was over, I needed traction – something that would pull me forward, not distraction. I thought when opening my deli that I had finally landed on my path – but that turned out a disaster, as I had started it for all the wrong reasons.

In a series of articles with the title "Change your box, change your reality" chiropractor, researcher, lecturer and author Dr Joe Dispenza wrote this on the use of futures thinking to pull you forward:

> "If you get really good at investing your energy into your future in the present moment, and thus your body starts following your mind to that future, wouldn't you agree when you start seeing all those wonderful synchronicities, coincidences, and serendipities in your life that you're going to keep doing it? And wouldn't you also agree that you're going to become more aware of your challenges, conditions, and tests when they are happening? Instead of falling for the

> trigger hook, line, and sinker, you're going to recognise when you've lost your state of being and switch right back into your heart."

When I was offered the opportunity to open a deli, I fell for the trigger hook, line and sinker. I only saw what my friend had and I wanted – but I didn't realise that what he had I couldn't achieve in the same way as he did. We weren't the same, and I wasn't aware of that.

When I became more aware of who I was and what I had in me that I could develop, and created my future on this knowledge, only then did I start to experience wonderful synchronicities, coincidences and serendipities. Through designing my life on purpose, I could then evolve on purpose, and started to recognise much more quickly when I felt out of sync. I've come to refer to the process as futurizing yourself and the benefits for health and wellbeing as the futures effect.

The futures effect being all the long-term, short-term and immediate benefits that are brought forth because you are using your futures skills on purpose.

Where does your attention lie? On this book, I hope. But step back a moment and become an observer of your attention. Is your attention focused in the past, present or future? Is it on others or on you? Is the place where your attention lies meaningful, or is it distracting you from greatness? There is a saying that I have mentioned before in this book: "Where attention goes, energy flows."

Do you want your energy to flow towards the future you want? Then futurize yourself: design your future wisely and make it work for you. Make it a focal point to which all your decisions, choices and actions are aligned. Design it based on your potential, which is what you actually have the capacity to develop into something and which is needed. It's a process – enjoy it. No, it will not always be a walk in the park, and you'll still face resistance and many challenges.

However, when you futurize yourself and start to evolve on purpose to have the GREAT future you want, you'll be able to know or find out why you are being challenged.

It's a bit like wanting to go to a particular place in the city but there is a roadblock in front of you and you're not sure how to proceed. In that moment, you can look for directions on a smartphone map app or just ask someone. The key is: you need to know where you are going.

This reminds me again of a passage from *Alice in Wonderland* where Alice asks the Cheshire Cat:

"'Would you tell me, please, which way I ought to go from here?'

'That depends a good deal on where you want to get to,' said the Cat.

'I don't much care where–' said Alice.

'Then it doesn't matter which way you go,' said the Cat."

Know where you are going, so that, when you are challenged, you can always question yourself. Question yourself, for example, by asking if what you are doing, or the situation you are in, is getting you to where you want to be. If not and you have deviated from your path, well, maybe it is very normal that things are complicated. That said, when you are still on track and things become complicated, challenging, or you feel that you're running against the current, well, you're probably evolving towards your next level – and with that, some resistance is normal.

One of the many benefits of futurizing yourself is that it helps you to evolve on purpose and be more aware of your evolution. At any moment, you can step back and become conscious of your situation by the act of self-distancing, and become your own observer. Did you know that when you adopt a self-distancing perspective, it can lower physiological distress and even impact your physical health positively (Özlem et al., 2010)?

From personal and professional experience, I can highly recommend that you stop and become your own observer on a regular basis. This means, in good and bad times, looking at yourself from a distance like an astronaut would look upon the Earth. You are, after all, a time-travelling astronaut who can see past, present and future scenarios all at once.

From a distance, you can become aware of the journey so far and glimpse the future you aspire to realise, and the present as the moment to evaluate where your attention lies – and also the moment where your decisions, choices and actions can make the difference to develop what you want into reality.

So, practically, to evaluate your evolution, you have to have an idea of what you want. Then, at any moment, you can stop, observe, interpret, and give yourself a good pat on the back when you are doing well, tell yourself to hang in there when you're facing resistance in your growth process, or realign with your purpose if the resistance you are feeling is due to your having deviated from your path.

Make sure, wherever you are, that you follow it up with action. It will be a waste of time if you just leave it at a Q&A session with yourself and then go and eat a sandwich.

Nor will it do you any good if you keep putting the blame elsewhere or keep worrying. Blaming someone else and worrying are both like a rocking chair: it gives you something to do, but it doesn't get you anywhere (a quote partly attributed to humorist Erma Bombeck).

You need to follow up by doing what will get you what the future you want on purpose. These are the decisions, choices and actions that will create your future experience. If it doesn't work, then review where you can do better through repeating steps two and three of futurizing yourself (See "Introduction: The benefits for y'our health and wellbeing").

At some point, you might need to revisit step one. Yes, there are limitations to this technique, so make sure that what the future you want is actually actionable – but more about that later. Now, let's continue our journey of embracing the future and making it work for you.

Being a pragmatic futurist

It's only too late if you don't start.

Tom Meyers

The future is unpredictable and will be what it will be. However, as I've been saying throughout this book and the previous one, that doesn't mean we can't anticipate the future or create scenarios of the future and work towards making these scenarios into an ongoing reality. A process that is not predicting the future but shaping the future so that it can shape you.

When I started to futurize myself, I had no idea that I was doing it. It just felt right, and when I started to see how my life changed for the better, I kept doing it. I never questioned it until others asked me about my story. Only when telling my story did I start to see how everything I had done and become had started with giving shape to my future. You could say that by giving shape to my future, my future had shaped me.

I also realised, as a result of talking to others, including futurists, that the future had never been something abstract but was, in fact, very concrete. Created into being through my decisions, choices and actions, the future became part of my present. Again, I wasn't aware of this at first, but it was working for me. I never questioned whether others were doing the same. I stopped comparing myself with others when I stopped living the dreams of others.

Now I recognise that what I have been doing all these years is putting into practice the theories and methods that professional futurists use to help organisations prepare for the future. The reason why organisations think about the future is to stay relevant and succeed in this fast-changing world. They know that if they keep doing what they've been doing all along, or doing it in the same way it has always been done, it will eventually lead to failure.

We human beings are each a living "organisation" of trillions of cells. Just like the organisations we have created, we live with and for others, compete with others and need others to survive. We live in that same fast-changing world in which we also want to be relevant and succeed. So, just like organisations, we need to anticipate probable, possible, plausible or preferable scenarios of the future, and then take action in order to prepare ourselves ahead of change. We – and that means each and every one of us, including you – need to think about y'our role in the future and prepare y'ourself for when the future becomes the present. Doing this will save a lot of stress and harm to your own health and wellbeing and that of the people around you.

What the future do you want? Here I am again, I know. I think you want to have a GREAT future. You want it to be good, resilient, evolvable, actionable and transcendent. So you can feel good, adaptable, flourish in the flow of evolution, and thrive in this fast-changing world and, through doing so, make the world a better place for yourself and future generations.

Yes, you can do this – because, between our ears, we humans have all that is needed to futurize ourselves. We have all it takes to think of the many scenarios of the future including possible, plausible, probable, preferable and projected futures.

When I first started futurizing myself and imagined my GREAT future, I didn't know what a wondrous, life-changing experience would result. Neither did I know about the theories and methods that can be used to think about the future, nor about the different scenarios of the future. All I wanted was to feel content, fulfilled and healthy. I wanted a good life and a sense that I was evolving somehow, growing, getting smarter and more complete with time, and being good at something. In short, I wanted to flourish and thrive, and I imagined a future where I was living in my element. So, when I was asked to imagine an ideal day in 10 years' time, I knew in my heart of hearts that it had to fill all the aforementioned boxes.

Designing my life on purpose was my answer. As I now look at my answer, I also realise that the future I envisaged included all the different (possible, plausible, probable, preferable and projected) future scenarios in one. Maybe one could say that, whether intuitively or by chance, I had created a holistic personal futures scenario.

Was it possible, plausible, or even probable that I could become a therapist who had developed his own approach and written a book about it and was asked around the world to give presentations and workshops? Yes, as I had not only found within me the potential of all these traits, but in a way, I had already expressed them – and when I had expressed them, I remembered having felt in my element, content, fulfilled and healthy, even if only for a moment. So when I projected living my potential, I couldn't imagine feeling anything other than at least the same as I had felt before. That was what I wanted. That was my preferable future, a future I positively hoped for. Today, and for some time now, my holistic future scenario has become my ongoing present.

It all depends on how you look at it. There is always room for improvement, and futurizing yourself is a pragmatic approach to life in a fast-changing and challenging world – not an exact science. For example, I didn't picture myself sitting here in this exact room, in this exact place with this exact laptop in front of me writing these exact words, but I have what I sought and intended to pursue. Do I feel complete? Completer than I was before, that is for sure. More content, more fulfilled and healthier too.

As I'm also evolving, over the years I have found other traits within that I'm called to develop further. Traits that could only manifest themselves after my initial five had their place and I was ready for them. This is the beauty of it. When you evolve on purpose, you develop and continue developing by discovering other traits that set in motion other discoveries, and so on. You never seem to arrive somewhere – and when you do, you never stay long. It's something I needed to learn and accept. See it as a process that you enjoy moment-to-moment and not at a specific point in time.

I do have to remind myself to enjoy the process now and then. Like most human beings, I am not hard-wired to enjoy the moment. By that, I mean that, from an evolutionary perspective, we are hard-wired to see danger and respond to immediate threats. This makes enjoying the moment possible – but as soon as the moment is gone, we are already thinking of the next challenge or problem. This is one of the reasons why it's so difficult to enjoy the process or the journey, but with practice and repetition, it can be learned. Our brains, unlike the brains of almost every other species, are prepared to treat the future as if it were the present (Gilbert, 2006).

This hard-wiring for immediate threats is also one of the reasons why we are not so good at responding to probable but distant dangers, like global warming. It creeps up on us slowly, in an initially non-threatening way. If I may make the comparison, it is like a back pain that starts with a bit of discomfort, but you dismiss it and hope it will go away. Meanwhile, you get used to the pain and don't do anything about it until a small, insignificant move has you stopped in your tracks and screaming with pain. Patients who come crawling into my practice often tell me that the pain they are experiencing started weeks ago. A pain that went away and then suddenly re-emerged with a vengeance. I think it probably didn't go away, but they got attuned to it, as it wasn't severe enough and thus could be ignored. I've been there, done that, got the T-shirt.

Anyway, where were we? Oh yes: being a pragmatic futurist who enjoys the process of evolving on purpose. I must admit, I count my blessings that I started futurizing myself more than 20 years ago, when life was still relatively simple. There is so much more at stake now. Maybe there always was a lot at stake. But only now do we feel and see it. We have seen with the COVID-19 pandemic how our behaviour matters. We are also experiencing the effects of climate change which are threatening millions of lives, plus we are all seeing how fast new technologies are emerging and influencing our private and working life.

Your life, health and wellbeing are at stake. We are faced with challenges so big that if we don't do anything now, there will only be a future for tardigrades. Yes, those "little water bears" that have survived exposure to outer space and are among the most resilient animals known to man.

Let's not wait before we do something about it. We, and I mean all of us, must think about what the future we want, and treat it as the present. We must think about uniting possible, plausible, probable, preferable and projected futures for the good of

Chapter 4: An Evolvable Future

mankind. To flourish and thrive, we need to incorporate futures thinking into all our decisions, choices and actions on purpose.

We all need to think ahead – not only about what we want, but our role in it and which steps we can take to make it happen. Make it happen so that all benefit. This is what futurizing yourself stands for.

We are relatively insignificant in global terms at the individual level. We need to turn our "Me" behaviour into "We" behaviour without losing sight of our individual strengths, role and evolution. Each and every one of us is unique, different, and that is our strength – and, together, we all need to play to our strengths to make the whole better.

As a wellbeing futurist, I share my story because I want to encourage and empower you in the present to make sure that you realise your power to create the future you want to see happen. Your contribution is important so that we can collectively flourish in the flow of evolution and thrive in this fast-changing world.

> The job of a futurist is not to say what is going to happen. The job of a futurist is to empower people in the present to create the future they want to see.
>
> (Rushkoff, 2018)

This requires a new mindset where, as author, teacher and documentarian Douglas Rushkoff (2018) says – in a conversation with Luke Robert Mason (Director, *Virtual Futures*) on "Why Futurists Suck" at Nesta's FutureFest 2018 – we see the word "future" as a verb, not a noun. The future is not some inevitability at which we arrive – it is something we make. According to Douglas Rushkoff, if we give up on the future as something that we're making in the present, then we've basically given up on free will and given up on humanity itself.

Powerful words. Seeing the future as a verb changes your perspective on life, don't you think? Futurizing yourself is the action you can take in the present to make the future you want, based on self-defined unwavering principles, into an ongoing reality.

The future is not far away – it is here in the making. Here and now. Not created by chance, but built on every decision and choice you make, all the actions you take or do not take, and the time left for you to make a difference.

Futurizing yourself is taking ownership of your future in the present, but for the good of mankind as a whole.

I know futurizing yourself isn't a walk in the park. But your life, health and wellbeing depend on it. Playtime has come and gone. Now let's step up and dedicate some of our time to shaping and creating the future we want – and, by doing so, we will evolve on purpose.

How to feel about the future

You get to choose how you feel... and shape your reality – it's the ultimate self-agency. Our feelings inform our thoughts. And our thoughts inform our behaviour.

Danielle Laporte

A lot has been said, so it's a good moment to stop and ask yourself: "How do I feel right now? How do I feel about the future?" and "Is how I feel what I want to feel?" Take a moment to think about this before continuing.

What do you want to feel? Have you ever asked yourself that question? I'm actually very curious how fast you came up with an answer and are able to define what you want to feel. Did you have an answer ready, or did you have to think about it? To make sure there is no confusion, the question is "What do you want to feel?" and not "How you are feeling?" (see Addendum for more information).

When patients walk into my practice, I usually know how they are feeling: not so well, otherwise they wouldn't be coming to see me. However, I do want to know what they want to feel. It is very curious to see that when I ask the "what" question, most often I get a long silence. If not for maintaining their health, most patients come to my practice because they are in pain. So what I expect them to say when I ask "What do you want to feel?" is "I don't want to feel pain any more" or maybe "I want to feel healthy and happy." But no…

Most patients look at me vacantly at first, and then their facial expression changes to one of surprise. They are surprised by the question and their own inability to respond. You can see in their eyes that they are experiencing some kind of network error. But that network error turns out to be very therapeutic, as not having an immediate answer to such an obvious question has triggered something within them. I know this because, at the next consultation, I often get to hear how my question had kept them occupied on the way home and for days afterwards.

So, what do you want to feel? Does this question trigger something in you? In any case, if you don't have an immediate answer, I urge you to ask yourself this fundamental and life-changing question: "What do I want to feel?" or "What do I want to feel on an ideal day?"

Once you have the answer, I'd like you to ponder on the following: "Is what you want to feel the same as what you wanted to feel 5 to 10 years ago?" and then: "Is this what you want/would like to feel in 5, 10… 30 years from now?"

To feel content, fulfilled and healthy – that is what I want to feel, wanted to feel, and how I would like to feel in the years to come – and I can't see that ever changing. The conditions and my environment will change, but these base feelings will always be part of what I want.

What I found out is that what I want to feel is timeless and ageless. I asked many patients about this and discovered it didn't matter who I asked – they all agreed. In other words, I had found a constant. You might think it's silly to pay so much attention to this, but think about it: how many constants do you have in your life? Constants that, even though the world is changing, will never change.

As we've seen already, you can build solid strategies around things that will be stable in time. Thus, feelings are something you can build on. If you are not sure how to answer the question "What the future do I want?" – well, maybe you can start by asking yourself: "What do I want to feel?" Then follow up with: "What do I need in order to feel that way?"

If there is anything you're going to remember and put into practice from this book, I hope this is part of it. So, please do think about what you want to feel. I believe it is probably the simplest way – although, again, it won't necessarily be easy – to experience the futures effect.

Why? Because, at the end of the day, isn't feeling what you want to feel a measure of a good life? I can't imagine anybody saying: "A good life is a life where I feel miserable." It's like somebody saying: "I'm going to watch a horror movie to relax."

So I would encourage you to include imagining what you want to feel – and always keeping this at the back of your mind – as you futurize yourself and shape y'our future through your decisions, choices and actions.

The Strange Order of Things

We are not thinking machines that feel; rather, we are feeling machines that think.

Antonio Damasio

Feelings are an important part of life and are different from emotions. Here is what I wrote about this in a blog post in March 2020:

> ### Feelings versus Emotions
>
> Feelings, yes, let's talk about our feelings and not about emotions for a change. Although they are closely linked with each other, there is, from a neuroscientific point of view, a difference that is interesting when you want to evolve on purpose.
>
> Feelings are mental experiences of body states. In other words, feelings are experienced from within, without (but not excluding) the need of a perceived-from-the-outside stimulus. For example, thirst, hunger and pain are all feelings. Anxiety, stress, happiness, contentment, fulfilment and love are also feelings that can be experienced without a visual, auditive or any other sensory stimulus.
>
> Emotions, on the other hand, are experiences mainly through our senses (vision, hearing, touch, taste and smell) and can trigger a feeling.
>
> In an interview with Scientific American Mind (2005) magazine, neurologist Antonio Damasio (a leader in understanding the biological origin of consciousness) explains: "When we are afraid of something we see our

hearts begin to race, our mouths become dry, our skin turns pale and our muscles contract. The emotional reaction (fear) occurs automatically and unconsciously. Feelings occur after we become aware in our brain of such physical changes; only then do we experience the feeling of fear."

Thus, note that we can experience fear as a feeling (conscious experience of the internal state) or an emotion (unconscious experience triggered by a fear-inducing sensory stimulus), but there is no different name for it – which makes it so damn complicated to keep feelings and emotions apart.

But why is this so important when you want to evolve on purpose? Yes, you may ask, and I will gladly tell you in the next blogs, as I'm still digesting the information I've gathered to support my feelings (pun intended).

My task over the next few days will be to make sense of the following:

"Evolving on purpose" is a conscious choice and feelings are conscious experiences.

Through feelings, we can construct ourselves (A. Damasio) and that means, for our purpose and reflection, that we can futurize ourselves through our feelings.

(Meyers, 2020)

If you are interested to know more about feelings and their evolution, I recommend you read *The Strange Order of Things* by neuroscientist Antonio Damasio (2018). A fantastic book, with many insights. For the purposes of this book and chapter, I've selected three statements for you:

"Feelings tell the mind, without any word being spoken, of the good or bad direction of the life process, at any moment, within its respective body. By doing so, feelings naturally qualify the life process as conducive or not to well-being and flourishing."

"Feelings work as motives to respond to a problem and as monitors of the success of the response or lack thereof."

"Feelings provide us with a moment-to-moment perspective on the state of our health."

Feelings motivate us, provide a moment-to-moment perspective on the state of our health, and qualify our wellbeing and flourishing. Your feelings are a tool for motivation, monitoring and mediation. I know – amazing, right? Because these are the tools needed to futurize yourself!

Simplified, it boils down to this: What you want to feel is your ultimate experience, your aim that you want to achieve. How you feel now is a consequence of the past up to this precise moment. Compare how you feel with what you want to feel. If there is a discrepancy, you've got some work to do.

Chapter 5:
An Actionable Future

When our over perfect demands upon ourselves, our idealised image of ourselves, break down under insight, the self-image of the perfect brave man, the perfect maternal woman, or the perfectly logical and rational person, collapses as we permit ourselves to discover our bits of cowardliness, envy, hostility or selfishness.

A.H. Maslow

Empowerment

It's up to you to take a chance or your life will never change.

Tom Meyers

Never in my wildest dreams did I imagine, when I designed my life and future on purpose, that I would one day actually live it. Yes, I could imagine that if I had the life I had envisaged, I would be content, fulfilled and healthy. But that was theoretical, and an imagined reality was not a reality I was sure to achieve.

From a "good for nothing" gourmet deli shopkeeper to a professional therapist seemed just impossible – let alone having developed my own approach, written a book and being asked to give presentations and workshops around the world.

But, as is so often the case, "It always seems impossible until it is done" (Nelson Mandela).

Fear of failure and limiting beliefs often play with our mind and keep us where we are. In my case, I was already a failure and thus had nothing left to lose when I started the journey. One could say that being at the bottom can have its advantages – if one hasn't lost hope and motivation, that is.

Although my hope and motivation were at an all-time low, I did manage to see a light at the end of the tunnel through the coaching I received. A light through the combination of three fundamental steps I had gone through. The first two steps were to get a new perspective on my past and to uncover my potential. Therapist, communicator, teacher, researcher and traveller – the unrealised talent I had uncovered became the foundation on which I could then build a narrative of a preferred future that made sense to me. A future that wasn't so alien, as it was built on what I could develop to reach my full potential and what I had already expressed but had never been aware of its significance.

Potential is often like that: it is there in plain sight, but you don't recognise it. Don't recognise it because you're not applying it every day or, just the opposite, you're so familiar with it that you don't consider it special or something unique. When I had created a talk on wine appreciation from scratch, organised and given a three-hour workshop on it without help, I didn't think that was special. I wanted to sell more wine, and this was a way to do it, I thought, so I just did it. Creating and writing the one-hour talk I would give was time-consuming, but fairly easy. The giving of the talk, something I had never done before, was nerve-racking at first, but once I was on a roll I was completely in my element, and people attending were very attentive during it and enthusiastic afterwards.

So, in that moment, I didn't think much about it at all. It only came back to me when I was figuring out what I had done so far where I thought and wished that I could do it forever.

Anyway – although I don't want to repeat myself, as you'll find the full story in my first book – finding my potential was a crucial part of my futurizing process, as the future I had designed was one which I considered – albeit with some reluctance – actionable.

I had already done it, so why couldn't I do it again and even do better? My reasoning didn't make my limiting beliefs of being good for nothing, someone who was never going to make it, go away. What it did do was it disarmed them enough to let hope through.

The whole process of futurizing myself created what I can only describe as a shift in my mindset. A shift where my future self rather than my past or present became my reference point.

My future self that I could evolve into became something to live for which transcended my past and my current situation and disarmed my limiting beliefs. Yes, I had doubts, but at the same time, what did I have to lose?

I also had it reinforced straight away that the path I had chosen was the right one. It truly is like Dr Joe Dispenza writes in Change the Box, Change Your Reality: Part III (2019): "If you get really good at investing your energy into your future in the present moment, and thus your body starts following your mind to that future, wouldn't you agree when you start seeing all those wonderful synchronicities, coincidences, and serendipities in your life that you're going to keep doing it? And wouldn't you also agree that you're going to become more aware of your challenges, conditions, and tests when they are happening?"

Yes and yes – and it's not only the synchronicities, coincidences and serendipities that will keep you going. When you futurize yourself and invest in your potential, you will experience moments where you feel in your element, a kind of easiness doing something although it might be the first time.

My first signs of that came during that first workshop to learn kinesiology I had enrolled in on my reconversion path. Not only did my first steps learning kinesiology feel like coming home; this was also reinforced by Agnes the instructor (as I explained earlier in this book).

Learning and practising kinesiology was the moment where my future self presented itself for the first time. This was where it was affirmed for me that the decision, choice and action I had undertaken to become a therapist was good and where my future became real. The future as in a verb which was playing itself out, something actionable and undeniable.

When I talk about the process of futurizing myself and creating and designing my life on purpose, I'm often asked how I knew that the future I had designed was the right one.

The double confirmation I just explained, where I not only felt at home but my feelings were reinforced by Agnes – that was how I knew I was on the right track. That was when I started to believe in the possibility of having what I longed for.

Here is another titbit of information good to know: I looked up to Agnes. She was who I wanted to be. A therapist with a private practice, a teacher and a communicator who had found herself.

When you look at these three observations – looking up to Agnes, being reinforced by her and feeling in my flow – doesn't that make you think of something? Indeed, they could be seen as the answers to the three questions (see my first book) that started my futurizing process.

Who did I look up to and why?
Agnes, the kinesiologist with her own private practice, who gave presentations and workshops.

For what advice or problems to solve did people come to me and not my friends?
She saw I had the potential and talent for it.

What had I done so far where I thought and wished that I could do it forever?
I felt I was in my flow when I was practising this manual healing approach, and I wanted more.

I'm just saying this to really show how important these questions have been – also afterwards. I've used them time and time again to uncover more of my potential, but they also helped me gain more confidence and assurance during the process of futurizing myself.

You might think now: "Tom, that second observation: that is not a straight answer to that second question." True, but with time I've learned to interpret all the questions a bit more broadly. It's not an exact science, but it comes down to this: with the first question, you observe the world around you; with the second, you can see yourself through the eyes of others, and the third is where you look within yourself.

So here for that second question, no, Agnes didn't come to me for help, but she did see something in me she didn't see in others. She didn't see it, for example, in the other person that was participating in the workshop. Or, at least, not that I know of.

When you are in your potential, you exude something that others can sense. Agnes saw and sensed something in me that stood out. I'm sure you can spot from afar people who are in their element, doing what they are born to do. This could be a person selling vegetables at a market, a cleaner or a mathematician.

We all have a unique blueprint in which we can be content, fulfilled and healthy that stands above the materialistic world and that has nothing to do with how much money we earn or have. So, just look around you and spot the people who are in their element.

At the same time, think about what people have recently commended you for or asked for your help with.

Exploring y'our future

You can't change the past, nor the present which happens too fast. For change, focus on creating a GREAT future and make it last.

Tom Meyers

When and where were you, and what were you doing, the last time you felt in your element? I hope your answer is here and now reading this book, as my sincere wish is that you are living a good and meaningful life in this very moment. A life where you are flourishing and thriving because you are developing your potential. A life where you have become resilient enough to cope and navigate this fast-changing world and are ready to face the multitude of changes and challenges, good or bad, that are ahead of you. A life where you are evolving into the best version of yourself and contributing to a world that is better because you are in it.

I sincerely hope that you have, or aspire to have, all the above and more. But I can imagine that, for some, this might all sound too good to be true. For some, it is hard to imagine that they can create a better world for themselves, let alone for all mankind. I know – I've been there. When I was dealing with some challenges in my life, I often felt that I had no control over the outcome. I believed that I was simply in the hands of outside forces.

But you will see that, once you start to futurize yourself and invest in your future self, things change. You will understand that there is more that you can control than you ever imagined was possible. The more engaged you are in creating an image of your future self and the more you pursue it, the more you'll be able to make the long-term decisions and choices and take the actions needed to make this future into an ongoing reality. Nobody can do this for you. You have probably heard the saying "If Not Me, Who? If Not Now, When?"

> For your information, it turns out this is a shortened version of:
>
> "If I am not for myself, who will be for me? If I am only for myself, what am I? And if not now, when?" (Hillel)

What the future do you want? Yes, I'm here again with that one question. Do you want a GREAT future, yes? What does that look like for you? What does that GREAT future look like with you in it? What are you doing, contributing to make the future GREAT?

All these questions boil down to the essence of life – of who you are. So, who are you? The question of all the ages, and one we struggle with. Why? Why do we struggle with this pertinent question? Do we lack the courage? Is the question too big? Or is it that we just didn't think of it? Didn't think of its importance? But I ask you, how will you create a GREAT future if you don't know yourself – or have a narrative for the future you want, for that matter? On what do you base your decisions, choices and actions if you don't know yourself or know where you are going? I know, I said it all before.

I just don't know you, the reader. I have an idea who you might be, and I can only imagine some of the challenges that you are experiencing, the questions, fears and hopes you may have. But exactly what you are experiencing, or where you find yourself on your journey, I have no idea. So, for some of you, I might sound repetitive. For others, for whom the emphasis I put on the importance of having a future narrative hadn't sunk in yet, I hope this reminder is valuable.

In this book, where I mainly focus on the years between designing my life on purpose and now, I see how that 20-plus years journey was characterised by getting to know myself better. Knowing what made me tick, what potential I had within me that could be developed into something, and knowing what I wanted. Finding out helped me to create a new narrative for my past and one for my future. These narratives made up the central principles of my behaviour and have been the key principles that helped me evolve on purpose into the GREAT life I so much longed for.

Principles guide behaviour

If we can recognise that change and uncertainty are basic principles, we can greet the future and the transformation we are undergoing with the understanding that we do not know enough to be pessimistic.

Hazel Henderson

Principles are like a mental framework that doesn't change over time and serves as the foundation for a belief or behaviour. I didn't know it at the time, but I need structure. I need something I can base my decisions, choices and actions on – a guide that I can fall back upon when needed. Something that is adaptable enough and can adjust to new conditions or that I'm able to modify to new demands. Principles do the trick for me. However, I can imagine that this is not everyone's cup of tea.

For those who know Insights® – the tool that helps people understand themselves better as individuals and leaders (www.insights.com) by using four colours to represent observable behavioural patterns – I'm predominantly blue (surprise, surprise!). Blue people are task-oriented introvert thinkers. They are strong in following processes and standards, and are usually strong in analytics, having an eye for the details. Their motto is "Let's do it correctly", and on a good day, blue people are formal, precise, careful and ask a lot of questions.

Principles motivate me and help me get a grip on the world and the future. I suppose, again without realising it at the time, principles are also one of the reasons why I fell in love with osteopathy.

For those who are not familiar with it, osteopathy is a

complementary hands-on treatment approach founded by Dr Andrew Taylor Still (Kirksville, Missouri, 1828–1917). Two principles were Dr Still's basis for osteopathy: cause and effect, and nature's unerring tendency towards health (Still, 1908). When these principles were properly applied, they enabled the blood and tissue to administer nature's perfect remedies, in the optimum dose and without side effects (Lewis, 2012). As a direct result of these principles, you can say that osteopaths do not cure disease; we correct the imbalances (lift the cause) so that the body can work normally (return to health).

- All diseases are mere effects, the cause being a partial or complete failure of the nerves to properly conduct the fluids of life.
- The rule of the artery is absolute, universal, and it must be unobstructed, or disease will result.

That said, the current practice of osteopathy is based on four fundamental principles to diagnose, treat and prevent illness and injury which are based on Dr Still's concepts and were set down as a study guide for osteopathy courses in 1953 by the Special Committee on Osteopathic Principles and Osteopathic Technic at Kirksville College of Osteopathy and Surgery.

These four principles are: (1) the body is a unit, (2) the body possesses self-regulatory mechanisms, (3) structure and function are reciprocally interrelated, and (4) rational therapy is based on an understanding of body unity, self-regulatory mechanisms, and the interrelationship of structure and function.

The osteopathy-based "Reaset Approach" that I developed and practise is based on all the above underlying principles and the therapeutic application of them united as one in the principle:

"Engagement – Stillpoint – Disengagement" or E**O**D in short.

You could say that the engagement phase is where I want to know what happened and why. I then follow its path in the body to come to the (still)points, where the imbalances are lifted and the body can return to health. The return to health being the disengagement (healing) phase that happens in the moment but, of course, often needs time. Healing is a continuous process and can take from a millisecond to hours, days or even months.

Hang on a minute… What do you know! Only now do I see that there is a relationship between the central principle of the "Reaset Approach" and "Futurizing Yourself". I just had this flashbulb-like experience that lights up my awareness and connects dots that I had never considered connecting. But now that I've become aware of it, it seems so obvious. So, hang on a minute so that I can get my head around it and put into words what I'm sensing at this very moment.

> Ever heard of "**felt sense**"? It's the name given by psychotherapist Eugene Gendlin (1966) to describe the unclear, pre-verbal sense of "something" – the inner knowledge or awareness that has not been consciously thought or verbalised – as that "something" is experienced in the body. Gendlin also described it as "sensing an implicit complexity, a wholistic sense of what one is working on."

How am I going to explain this? OK, so I was saying that everything changed for me when I had created a new narrative for my past, got to know myself (found my potential) and created a narrative for my future. In other words, there are three phases: past, present and future.

As I mentioned before, in the Reaset Approach there are three phases: the engagement, stillpoint and disengagement phases.

The engagement phase is that part where I as an osteopath listen and try to find out the symptoms (effect) with which the patient needs help and what caused them. It is that part where I try to establish an image of the patient's health. This state evolved from what was before to that moment of listening. In other words, in the engagement phase we listen and learn from the patterns created up till that moment.

But that is not all. During the engagement phase, I also take time to listen with my hands. Through touch, I become aware of what the body has to say. I feel and follow the flow in the structure of the body. In my mind, I'm looking for health, and when there is a deviation from health, I pay close attention to the patterns that present themselves, and passively assist these patterns to where they want to go without consciously interfering.

Just like the patient's verbal story, the body tells a story too, and together they form a narrative of the past. Permit me to give an example.

A patient comes in and explains they are suffering from neck and shoulder pain. I ask if it is a dull or sharp pain, when it started, and what they were doing when they first felt it.

After this initial anamnesis, I ask the patient to lie down on the osteopathy table and, when settled in comfortably, I place my hands under and on the head, neck and shoulders. I explore each region and I indeed feel the tension that has built up over time.

Osteopathy is a whole-body approach, so I not only look at the area with the symptoms but also explore the arms, hands, thorax, abdominal cavity, legs, feet, craniosacral system, etc.

At the ankle, I also feel tension, and I feel that the foot is starting to move inward spontaneously. A sprain that hasn't healed properly? The patient hadn't said anything about this, as they had forgotten about it – however, the body hadn't. When asked about the possibility of a recent ankle sprain, the patient answers: "Yes, I forgot to tell you. It happened while running, but it doesn't hurt any more."

It happens more than you might think that people forget to mention a recent fall, or a pain that has been there so long, that they have got so used to it – it is filtered out of their consciousness. Osteopaths are like researchers or detectives with a nose for unearthing the truth, trained to feel the narrative of the past that hasn't healed properly, even if the patient has forgotten about it or filtered it out.

To come back to the ankle: why is this important? Because, as an osteopath, I know that this asymptomatic ankle problem could have led or contributed to the neck and shoulder problems. If this is the case, I need to treat it too, to bring the patient relief from their neck and shoulder pain. If it hasn't contributed, well, I need to treat it too, because it might lead to problems later that can be prevented. Every deviation from the norm is thus treated.

As regards the treatment part of the Reaset Approach, this is not something I do separately. By this I mean that, wherever I feel an imbalance, a deviation from normal functioning, I continue to follow and assist the tissues that have the unerring tendency towards health. I follow until the stillpoint – the point where the balance is restored, i.e., reaset, and the tissues can return to ease. Thus, the third phase, the disengagement phase where the body starts to relax, recuperate and regenerate, sets in. While the reaset sets in immediately, it is not always the case for the recuperation and regeneration, i.e., healing of the tissues or system.

This healing, as you well know, can take some hours, days or even weeks and is also dependent on the environment the patient goes back to. So, in other words, the actual healing happens in the future.

> I want you to imagine you are holding someone's foot. The person has recently twisted their ankle. It was just a little slip, without causing any swelling. The pain has since subsided. You are holding their twisted foot in both hands, with the toes pointing towards you. Let's say it is the right foot. So your right hand will be holding the inner side of the foot and your left hand the outside. Don't press; take hold of it as lightly as possible. What do you think a normal, uninjured foot would feel like? Unlike what you might think, it is not nothing that you will feel. The foot is alive, full of blood rushing through it, and a zillion other processes are taking place. What you will feel is a summary of all this activity, which presents itself as a slight rocking movement that you can become aware of. This is what you are looking for, but this will be absent when a twisted foot hasn't reaset itself to health. Instead of the rocking feeling, you will feel the ankle rolling inwards. It has held the memory of the slip.
>
> Now, don't take your hands away. Just keep following that

> movement until the end and the movement stops. That is your stillpoint right there. That is where, in that very present-moment, the reaset happens and tissues can return to ease so that the third phase can take place.

The future (which will become the present) is the patient's ongoing process of returning to health – what the patient and I want and the objective of the treatment. An objective that is held with intention and attention from the moment a patient walks into my practice until they walk out, and thus held throughout the EOD phases.

Just as you have to know what the future you want when futurizing yourself, so I need to know what the future the patient wants and what I want for them in the Reaset Approach.

With what I've just written, I hope I've been able to put my sudden insight into words. Insight on the aspects of past, present and future, with the future as the key, that I so clearly saw in the concept of Futurizing Yourself – but I hadn't realised how all the timeframes are also present, with the future the key aspect, in the Reaset Approach. In any healing approach, for that matter, the future should be the sole objective. If it isn't, change your doctor or therapist quickly.

Time is key to understanding y'our evolution

For the first time in human evolution, the individual life is long enough, and the cultural transformation swift enough, that the individual mind is now a constituent player in the global transformation of human culture.

William Irwin Thompson

So what, Tom, that past, present and future are to be found in the Reaset Approach and in Futurizing Yourself, or that the key is the future in both? Why is this so important? Yes, you may ask. I'm actually wondering about the same thing myself. But again, I find myself drawn to stop and ponder about this by my felt sense. That the future is guiding my world in more ways than I imagined up until now is one thing, but I sense there is more to unearth.

More – and I feel in my heart, body and soul that it is important, but I can't put my finger on it yet. So here I must ask you again, dear reader, to bear with me to let me crystallise these feelings into comprehension and, hopefully, words.

Like the mythological emissary and messenger Hermes, I need to cross boundaries and let my mind wander and transduce what is intangible – but within me, and make it concrete here in writing.

There is more but, er, I'm drawing a big blank... no words are coming. So I'll let it sit for a while so my brain can consolidate the information. I'll be back; time for a coffee, methinks.

OK, while pottering about in my practice slurping a coffee, the reflection that came up was whether time is an illusion, as Einstein wrote. Or does time exist? Searching the internet, I found an interesting transcription of a conversation in which theoretical physicist Lee Smolin disagrees with Einstein. Smolin thinks time is real and considers it a key to understanding the evolution of the universe (NPR, 2013).

That statement, that time is key to the understanding of evolution, caught my attention. Because, with my puny brain, I wonder if – following Smolin's argument – we could deduce that time is also key to understanding our – humans' – evolution, as we are part of the universe. Seems logical to me.

I'm sure you'll agree that, over time, we've made time real. Today, we have clocks, and we can look back to what we have done before and look ahead to what we want – and do all of that in the ongoing present. We can conjure up past, present and future, we can schedule meetings, and have a sense of time – all in the ongoing moment. Although there is only the now, that doesn't mean there wasn't yesterday or there won't be tomorrow. Time is more than the sum of its parts. Just as we are more than the sum of our parts – body, mind and spirit.

But how much have we truly considered the future in the equation of our time – and our identity, for that matter? On the Unholy podcast, I heard historian and author Yuval Noah Harari say: "Our identities are not just about the past; they are equally about the future" (Levi and Freedland, 2021).

Who we are and what we are depends on our future, on what we want and who we want to be. However, as I've mentioned before in this book, although we do consider our immediate future, we've mostly ignored the long-term future, as we are primed to focus on our immediate needs.

Y'our brain has evolved to manage the needs of the now and tomorrow, but not y'our distant future. The distant future is uncertain, and uncertainty creates stress. So why go there?

Chapter 5: An Actionable Future

"Better to focus on the now – it's safer!" Well, it might have been a lifesaver for the prehistoric man, woman and child – but today, ignoring y'our future is a deadly game.

Just look at climate change. If we don't start doing something now, it will be too late. Too late for whom? For you…

> "Climate change has long been misunderstood as an environmental issue affecting the survival of the planet. The truth is, the planet will continue to evolve."
>
> "The planet will survive, in changed form no doubt, but it will survive. The question is whether we will be here to witness it."
>
> (Figueres and Rivett-Carnac, 2020)

We've mainly considered the future as a continuation of the past, but that has got us into a bit of a pickle, wouldn't you say? It's a bit like the pickle we got ourselves into when scientists considered mind and body as separate (dualism), finding resolution when we brought them back together (monism). Then scientists saw that, if you just looked at the role of the body and the mind in relation to health, disease and human development, something was still missing. Some understood the importance of social aspects and added them to the equation. More recently, some are also connecting spirit. Thus, we realise we are of one in body, mind and spirit, within a social context. In science, they speak of the biopsychosocial-spiritual health and wellbeing model. Please check it out in your favourite web browser.

Back to our past, present and future. We've been focused on the present and our not-so-distant future. We've mainly seen the future as a continuation of our past. We did – and do – this because we feel more at ease and secure keeping the status quo – and life – within what is predictable. That was all well and good when our environment was evolving more slowly than, or at the same pace as, we were. That time has come and gone.

Our environment is evolving faster than we are. We can't ignore our distant future any more. Today it is essential to consider the long-term consequences of our decisions, choices and actions. Not doing so will be disastrous for our health and wellbeing, to put it really mildly. To put it strongly: ignoring our future will kill many of us, if not all of us, over time. Is that what you want? Is that what you want for your children or your children's children?

Futurizing yourself and including y'our long-term future in your decisions, choices and actions is not only a stress-management technique. More importantly, y'our health and wellbeing – y'our survival – depend on it.

Health and wellbeing depend on body, mind, spirit and y'our social environment.

Health and wellbeing also depend on how you deal with the past, the ongoing present, y'our future and spacetime, as we are as one traversing the cosmos. Spacetime is important. Just look at astronauts who age a tiny bit more slowly than we do here on Earth. Because, depending on our position and speed, time can appear to us to move more quickly or more slowly relative to others in a different part of spacetime (time dilation). I can't get my head around this. Apparently, it has something to do with gravity and can be explained by Einstein's theory of relativity.

For that matter, y'our health, wellbeing and future also depend

Chapter 5: An Actionable Future

on y'our position in space, y'our spatial environment. As above, so below, so to speak! Well, yes, we are not the only moving rock orbiting elliptically around the Sun and making a journey through the galaxy. Some other bigger and smaller rocks are traversing space too. These include, for example, asteroids. You might have heard of them.

However, unlike in the time of the dinosaurs, some clever people have now mapped out the size and speed of most of these rocks.

By the way, did you know that about 5,200 tonnes of micrometeorites fall to Earth every year (Derouin, 2021)? I know – amazing, right? Micrometeorites aren't a problem and can't be mapped; nor are the sizeable chunks of space debris that appear as brilliant shooting stars. However, a rock the size of a house or bigger coming our way will definitely be a problem – so, now that we can, mapping them is essential. Now we just need to hope that we will be ready to do something about it in time when a sizeable one does come our way.

> I highly recommend you take the time to watch the film *Don't Look Up* directed by Adam McKay. The film is about two low-level astronomers who have to go on a giant media tour to warn mankind of an approaching comet that will destroy Planet Earth.

Luckily, we have NASA for this. Clever people at NASA have come up with a solution, a Double Asteroid Redirection Test (DART). They not only came up with it but also developed it –

and successfully used it to alter an asteroid's orbit on 26 September 2022 (Tavernier, 2022). A project that was approved in August 2018 and thought up many moons before that. I'm just making the point that looking a long time ahead, and creating possible, probable and plausible scenarios, does matter. Y'our health and wellbeing – and your survival – will be more secure as a result.

Past, present, future; engagement, stillpoint, disengagement; body, mind, spirit – they are all one. They are all of one, and together they become more than the sum of their parts. Both in applying the Reaset Approach, where healing the patient is the objective, and in futurizing yourself, where creating a GREAT future in which you can flourish and thrive is the objective, it is the future that is used to determine decisions, choices and actions.

I see it clearly and understand now what my innate wisdom was trying to tell me. **We are living in a time where neither past nor present, but the future has become the key to y'our health and wellbeing and the wellbeing of our planet on which we depend.** With our survival at stake, we can't afford not to think about our long-term future. **The future is life – as, without the future, there is no (room for) life.**

Don't be scared – be prepared for the future

The pace of change has never been this fast, yet it will never be this slow again. There's enormous opportunity, and enormous potential, in that realisation.

Justin Trudeau

Let's get back to the essence here. Who are you? What the future do you want? How do you want to feel on an ideal day? What do you need to have or do in your life to feel how you want to feel?

I sincerely hope that your answer is: "I want to feel content, fulfilled and healthy." Don't you? We may have our differences, but I believe that we share these unwavering feelings. That we share at least wanting to feel content, fulfilled and healthy. But please correct me if I'm wrong.

I also think that, deep down, whatever our differences – age, gender, culture or part of the world you are from – you want to have or contribute to a good, resilient, evolvable, actionable and transcendent – in other words, GREAT – future. A future where you flourish and thrive because you are in your element doing what you were born to do. A future where you are navigating the changes ahead with ease, feel you are developing into the best version of yourself, where your actions matter – and a future where all beings, including future generations, can have a GREAT future too.

Y'our future depends on what you do today, and what you do today depends on y'our memories and assumptions about the future. Maybe – like me so many moons ago – you haven't really thought about this. Haven't thought that you could have more say over your future and, by taking responsibility for your actions, steer your future and even be ahead of the future. The future is y'our future.

Please reflect on this statement by the Director of Teach the Future Mexico, Professor Alethia Berenice Montero Baena:

> "If the past has come and gone and the present is happening too fast, well, you still have the future to change, to improve, to generate opportunities that best suit you – with yourself, the surroundings and with others."

I know, I know… I see with my patients how difficult it is to envisage the future and define what you want, especially when there is so much uncertainty and insecurity around.

However, just like I do for my patients, I'd like to make it easier for you. I'd like to make futurizing yourself easier and actionable by sharing my experience and thoughts, but also by giving you an adaptable framework you can start with and build on.

But to do that, we first need to agree on a few points.

Do you agree that, like me and all the patients I've asked so far, you want to feel content, fulfilled and healthy for evermore? So far, I haven't met anybody who didn't want this.

Secondly, do you want a GREAT future? Again, I haven't met anybody yet who didn't want this.

Yes to both? Then we are of one mind, and you too have your first, let's call them, resolute unchangeable ideals, the two strands of the DNA-like structure – the "why" you can build on as you begin to evolve on purpose.

Now add to this structure your potential, the skill set, the ladder

Chapter 5: An Actionable Future

of the DNA-like structure, the "what" you were born with – which also doesn't change. Add them as building blocks on which you can construct and create a GREAT future.

FEELINGS   POTENTIAL   ASPIRATIONS

Depiction of "Your DNA for the Future" by Tom Meyers

In the example here below, I have added my own "DNA for the Future" with, on the left (strand), what I want to feel; on the right (strand), my aspirations; and, in the middle, my potential (bonds).

CONTENT	THERAPIST	GOOD
FULFILLED	COMMUNICATOR	RESILIENT
HEALTHY	TEACHER	EVOLVABLE
	RESEARCHER	ACTIONABLE
	TRAVELLER	TRANSCENDENT

So, what do you want to feel and aspire to in the future you want? You can use what I want to feel and aspire to as a starting point, but please think about it first and change or complete the lists. Then, add your potential (see my previous book) and put the keywords in the middle. Now you have your "DNA for the future".

CONTENT	_____	GOOD
FULFILLED	_____	RESILIENT
HEALTHY	_____	EVOLVABLE
...	_____	ACTIONABLE
	_____	TRANSCENDENT
		...

From now on, you can start using your "DNA for the future" as one constant, unwavering **"organising principle"** (O) to futurize yourself on purpose. An organising principle to which you can align your short, medium and long-term decisions, choices and actions.

But not only that: When faced with a challenge or challenges, when the going gets tough, you can use these resolute unwavering ideals as a **"guiding principle"** (G) to see if the challenge or the resistance you are facing is because you have deviated from your ideals – from the future you want – or whether this challenge is part of a process for you to grow into the best version of yourself. So, once your ideals have been set, at any given moment you can evaluate and steer yourself.

Thirdly, these resolute unchangeable ideals can be used as a **"development principle"** (D), as, for the brain, they can provide a means of certainty – which is needed in order to evolve. The human brain is an "anticipation machine" and "making [the] future" is the most important thing it does (Grupe and Nitschke, 2013). Uncertainty about the future can paralyse you (freeze mode) and disrupt your ability to think constructively about the future. It can also disrupt your ability to avoid that unwanted future, resulting in that future becoming a self-fulfilling prophecy.

The future is intrinsically uncertain, but, by proactively using resolute unchangeable ideals, you will always have anchor points which you can fall back on. Knowing that you have something to fall back on lessens the insecurity and uncertainty about the future, because you have created a safety net.

Yes, you will, through your own proactive actions, manage the uncertainty, stress and anxiety that might occur in difficult or challenging moments – that surely will arise. You will prevent certain situations from paralysing you, while increasing the odds for your desired outcome.

Yes, you could say that these resolute unchangeable ideals are a preventive, future-oriented stress management tool. The more efficient and effective you become at preparing for the future, the less stress and anxiety you will experience – or, in the words of Global Futurist and Founder of Silicon Humanism, Sylvia Gallusser: "Don't be scared – be prepared for the future."

For me, establishing these resolute unchangeable ideals, and using them as a guiding (G), organising (O) and development (D) principle, was a lifesaver. In my moment of crisis, to have this unwavering structure I believed in, aimed for and could fall back on became like an anchor point or, better, a backbone I could rely on, to weather the changes and challenges of the moment and ahead, and also to deal with my fear of failure. Ever since, I've used the same G.O.D. principle to weather the many changes and challenges this fast-changing, volatile, uncertain, complex and ambiguous (VUCA) world has thrown at me.

When I was struggling business-wise or was challenged by exams, illness, deception, disappointment or being laid off, and during the pandemic, I always faced these challenges by first remembering what I wanted. Then seeing what I could learn, and what I could do, through my decisions, choices and actions, to have or stay in line with what I wanted. Every time I grabbed back to my unwavering ideals and narrative for the future to cope, understand, hold on and move on.

Try it…

Chapter 5: An Actionable Future

The future matters

Our future self is the beneficiary or unfortunate inheritor of all our major decisions and daily choices.

Ganschow et al.

We are living in an era of global disruption, a time where climate change, automation, datafication and so many megatrends are changing how we live and go about our lives. There is no escaping the fact that we are living in an era where the evolution of technology has outpaced y'our own evolution. In the midst of a crisis, you might think me non compos mentis when I say this, but to make decisions and choices with a longer future in mind is exactly what you need to take time for – it is what needs to be done.

I know that, when upheaval reigns, making long-term future plans seems virtually impossible. When uncertainty reigns, or during or just after a particularly stressful or painful situation, making plans for the future might even feel inappropriate.

I remember when my deli was failing, and I with it, that making future plans was far from my mind. I'm sure that, if I hadn't been told to do so, I would never have thought about it. First of all, there were more pressing problems that kept me bound to the present. I had no time for the future. Secondly, the only future I could imagine was a future according to the worst possible scenario. A scenario where I would never be good at anything, I wouldn't make it, and for sure I wouldn't find happiness, fulfilment, joy, success or love, and so on.

On the other hand, when it came to sulking about the past and loathing the present, that was something I had no problem doing. It also got me nowhere – except deeper down the rabbit hole.

On another, deeper level, there was also a conflict raging within the conflict. Some part of me knew what it wanted, even knew what I needed to do, while another part leaned towards accepting my current fate and accepting that, no matter what I might try, there was nothing that could be done about it.

Mechelen, 28 January 2000

The urge to wander fills my heart and soul. I want that feeling again of being free as I feel now trapped between these walls. What have I done?

I know the grass is not always greener on the other side and I realise if my wishes were met I could wander again tomorrow. But I would be running away again and I would keep on running.

Then, on the other hand, I might find what I am looking for. I might find myself there somewhere. Find the person that I'm supposed to be. I want to be able to look in that mirror again and say: "I know you, I love you, you're me." But now all I see is a body with eyes that only represent the emptiness that can be found beyond them. The emptiness is the soul that brings up these thoughts and that analyses that shape that represents itself in the mind. But you're writing. No, I am not. That hand just writes what it thought to write. It doesn't belong to me.

What has happened to me? Why are my body and soul not vibrating on the same level? Why do I feel so lost in this strange fishbowl we call Earth? Why do I feel I'm not walking at the same speed as others do? Why do I feel so detached from the world outside?

I wish I could understand. I have to learn to understand as otherwise, I will tumble off that narrow ledge I've been walking upon. What has stopped me before from letting myself fall doesn't hold me back any more as it doesn't exist any more. There are no more debts or responsibilities to anyone. To myself, I have none anyway. What stops me is fear. Fear that my soul will live on in torture. I hate pain. But, believe me, I am not far from total failure. I even have already chosen the way. Just a small push and I will not fear any more as I would not care.

As you can read in the lines above, I experienced a deep internal conflict, and my thoughts and outlook on life were very bleak at the time. But when I read between the lines, I see that, deep down, something in me was trying to let itself be heard. Was this my soul? This extract from my diary was from before. From before I was shown how to futurize myself and change from within.

In another diary entry, with the date unknown but probably September 1997, and which you can find in Chapter 1 of my first book in the section "Lost and found and lost again", I wrote:

"The problem is the subconscious, the core of the onion that I cannot remember the significance of." And: "The mere fact of knowing, plus proper guidance, might relieve me, or at least take my anxiety down to an acceptable level."

This was written after experiencing a major breakdown while working as a supervisor on the cruise ship, the Queen Elizabeth 2. So this was three years before the previous excerpt – and, again, I'm amazed at how lucid and true these words are.

I was scared of the future – why? I was scared because the only future I could imagine was more of the same. More of the same patterns that had presented themselves so far, and in ever shorter cycles. I couldn't imagine that ever changing – the natural flow of things that I was fated to experience.

Little did I know at the time that the way to break the downward cycle was to get proper guidance to find my core. I believed that I didn't need help and that no one could help me. I wasn't able to help myself, so why would somebody else be able to do so? I suppose that I also had a wrong image of what "help" was. All the coaching and therapy in the world hadn't helped my mother, so why would it help me?

Still, I did try, and I saw that it worked – and I advise you to give it a chance if you are in doubt.

The future reimagined

We can only move forward in time, we can only fully be understood as beings continuously in the process of becoming.

Jennice Vilhauer

In an article entitled 'Looking Back From the Future: Perspective Taking in Virtual Reality Increases Future Self-Continuity' (Ganschow et al., 2021), we read: "Our future self is the beneficiary or unfortunate inheritor of all our major decisions and daily choices. During these choices, the tendency to act for the benefit of the future self has been shown to be contingent upon the degree of connection between the person's present and future selves, or future self-continuity. These choices tend to accrue over time with future self-continuity positively correlating with better general well-being, improved mental health, better academic performance, and greater personal net worth. Importantly, an emerging body of evidence has shown that experimentally increasing future self-continuity in the present can also influence future-oriented behaviors contingent to these outcomes, such as increased exercise duration, promoting ethical decision making, reducing procrastination, and increasing savings behavior."

> **Future Self-Continuity**
>
> The extent to which individuals feel connected to and compatible with their future selves (Oyserman, 2009).

Yes, as you can see above, even science has caught on to the benefits of futures thinking for your health, wellbeing and more.

In a study from 2020 by Polk et al., it was found that people who balance living in the moment with planning for the future are best able to weather daily stress without succumbing to negative moods, as making plans also helps the brain to focus and come up with solutions.

"Energy flows where attention goes" is not just a pretty quote – it is reality. So, yes, as bonkers as it sounds to think about the future, what seems impossible to do is exactly what is needed in these fast-changing and challenging times.

The attentive reader might now say: "Oh, wait a minute… in Chapter 3 you say that your brain is not wired for futures thinking, and also you wrote that your brain starts acting as if you're thinking about a stranger when you imagine your future self, especially the further into the future you go." Yes – and, yes, I also wrote: "the more disconnected you are from your future self – the less motivated you will be to plan for your future."

So the key is to get connected to your future self to create future self-continuity. An emerging body of evidence has shown that increasing your future self-continuity in the present influences your future-oriented behaviour and creates the belief in the stability of your "self" over time. In other words – and this has also been my personal experience: futurizing yourself has all the elements to create the stability and security you need to overcome the uncertainty and stress about the future.

Chapter 6:
A Transcendent Future

Try and leave this world a little better than you found it, and when your turn comes to die, you can die happy in feeling that at any rate, you have not wasted your time but have done your best.

Baden-Powell

Being a good ancestor

Be a good ancestor. Stand for something bigger than yourself. Add value to the Earth during your sojourn.

Marian Wright Edelman

Have you ever thought of the world you inherited or the world you will leave behind?

The world you were born into was built on the sum of the consequences of the decisions, choices and actions of many individuals of times gone by. Those individuals include your family but also every single person that lived before you.

How do you feel about the world you inherited? Are you glad or sad? Maybe you are indifferent because "it was what it was, so what's the point of thinking about it?" Where you and we all come from matters. It has shaped us into who we are today, and it steers y'our future. However, as explained in this book, y'our past and y'our present don't have to define y'our future. We owe it to our future self, who is "the beneficiary or unfortunate inheritor of all our major decisions and daily choices" (Ganschow et al., 2021) but also, and consequently, to the future of generations to come.

Let me ask you another question. How much has the world changed since you entered it? Are you happy with the way the world has evolved and where it is going? Are you happy with your evolution? Was your life meaningful, did you become a better person, and would you consider yourself a good ancestor – someone who is contributing to leaving the world a better place than when you entered it? Would others be of one mind with you? Would future generations see you as a good ancestor?

Chapter 6: A Transcendent Future

I must admit I don't want to spend too many words on this chapter. However, the fact that I'm not writing many words about this subject does not mean that it is any less important. Far from it! As Jonas Salk (1914–1995), the American virologist who developed the first polio vaccine, said: "Our greatest responsibility is to be good ancestors."

I wholeheartedly believe that. Although I must admit it was only recently that I became aware that I have such a responsibility. Maybe it is because, having crossed the cap of 50, I have entered a stage of life where one thinks a bit more about the next generation.

That personal aspect aside, when I started to think about the unwavering principles and resolute unchangeable ideals, I realised that, when our time has come, we want to leave this world a little better than it was when we entered it. It is part of who we are.

Apart from that deep desire, it is a fact that what we now think of as the far-off future will one day become the present for someone, and we will be considered as ancestors. As our forebears have influenced the way we live today, so we are also influencing generations to come. This is an aspect of life that we often go to great lengths to evade. However, thinking about it actually makes us better humans.

Transcending the self has been a key message throughout this book, as it is an integral part of long-term futures thinking. I believe that this is a part of the process of futurizing yourself that adds to the aspects of meaning and purpose, and contributes to the decisions and choices we need to make that will change the way we act.

Remember, every decision and choice you make, and every

action you take, has an impact on others, and vice versa. "Others" also includes future generations... We are as much connected with the past as we are with the future. The COVID-19 pandemic has made it very clear how past, present and future are linked; may this be a lesson to live in the present but with tomorrow in mind.

What we do today matters. Our individual decisions, choices and actions matter – but a GREAT future cannot be reached alone, as we are not alone. But we seem to take it all for granted. Take for granted not only how much we rely on one another, but also how much influence we have on others and generations to come. It can be overwhelming – but, again, thinking about your legacy can make you a better human being and contribute to long-term meaningful change.

So, when considering what the future you want, please make sure you don't forget that, for you to feel content, fulfilled and healthy and have a GREAT future where you flourish and thrive, you are dependent on others, just as others depend on you. Y'our GREAT future also depends on the health and wellbeing of the planet.

Let me leave you with some inspiring words:

From Jonas Salk, the man who developed the polio vaccine:

> "Will future generations speak of the wisdom of their ancestors as we are inclined to speak of ours? If we want to be good ancestors we should show future generations how we coped with an age of great change and great crises."

Chapter 6: A Transcendent Future

From Roman Krznaric, the author of *The Good Ancestor: How to Think Long-Term in a Short-Term World* (2021):

> "In an incredibly short period of time we have endangered a world that took billions of years to evolve. We are just a tiny link in the great chain of living organisms, so who are we to put it all in jeopardy with our ecological blindness and deadly technologies? Don't we have an obligation, a responsibility, to our planetary future and the generations of humans and other species to come?"

And, finally, from John Green, the author of *The Fault in Our Stars* (2014):

> "We all want to make a contribution and leave our mark. How do you do that in a meaningful way? But searching for such answers is a side effect of another underlying belief: that there is an answer at all. Maybe there is no answer. The world is a pretty absurd place. And unfortunately, there's no roadmap, but rather hints and clues along the way."

The Futures Effect

Chapter 7:
Your Future Self

A meaningful life can be extremely satisfying even in the midst of hardship, whereas a meaningless life is a terrible ordeal no matter how comfortable it is.

Yuval Noah Harari

Embracing your future self

Close the gap between your future self, what the future you want and where you/we are today. Your future self will thank you for it.

Tom Meyers

Neither past nor present but the future has become the key to y'our existence. Today, y'our future should become your primary objective to which you align your decisions, choices and actions. That is assuming that you, like me, aspire to have a GREAT future – a future worth living that future generations will also thank you for. Because, if we continue to behave this way and continue to turn a blind eye to our future and leave it up to chance, we – humanity – will suffer a great deal. We might even not survive for very much longer. Without action, Earth is headed for well over two degrees of warming if we don't change our habits. 2021 was already the warmest year on record, with 0.85 degrees Celsius above the average baseline of 1951–1980.

I can imagine that some of you, while reading the above, think that I should be a bit more optimistic and rely on new technological developments to do the trick. Others might think: "I'm just one person, I can't make a difference" or: "Individuals aren't to blame; corporations and governments are." The real pessimist might even think: "It's too late, anyway, to change anything. Que Sera, Sera!"

Thoughts I can well understand. But do you think, with all that we know, see and experience today, that it won't get out of hand? That the United Nations, the World Economic Forum, the World Health Organization, UNESCO and many other organisations are all barking up the wrong tree?

I know it is difficult to grasp – but what if it is true? What if it is true that humanity will become extinct through our own doing, unless we change our behaviour, and that this is the decisive decade? Decisive for us and many other species, but not for Planet Earth itself, which will continue to journey through the cosmos just as it has done after the last five major extinction events.

It also might not be in your lifetime that we will become extinct, but rather in the lifetime of your children or your children's children. Maybe it will happen not by our own doing but by some planet-killer asteroid hitting us, like in the film *Don't Look Up*.

The fact is that a wide range of future scenarios are possible, from the dystopian to the utopian. What the future will look like, we don't really know; there are numerous possible futures. However, the good news is that you can imagine and create scenarios of the future and envisage what you want the preferred future to look like. Yes, you can treat yourself the way your future self would want you to be treated. You can also steer and nurture the future in the present in a way that will help to avoid unwanted scenarios. All this you can do by thinking of your future self, committing to it, by making conscious decisions and choices and by taking appropriate actions with y'our future in mind.

You can, but are you doing so? I hope so – or I hope I've given you reason to, and a bit of how to do it, starting today. There are nothing but benefits to adopting a futures mindset. Benefits to y'our health and wellbeing, y'our quality of life in y'our evolution, and benefits for our planet on which we depend.

Futurizing Yourself is evolving on purpose, which is key to flourishing and thriving in this world that is evolving faster than we are.

Yes, we are evolutionarily hard-wired to respond to short-term problems, and naturally disposed to disregard issues that are in the distant future, issues that are not challenging our daily lives or those which dilute our convenience.

Yes, "We tend to make decisions with consequences that are pleasant in the present but harmful in the future. We eat fast food rather than vegetables, watch TV rather than exercise, spend rather than save, and otherwise choose immediate gratification over long-term benefit because we feel disconnected with our future self." (Rutchick et al., 2018)

Yes, "The future self being is a stranger to us at a neural level the further in the future we imagine ourselves" (Hershfield, 2011; Brietzke & Meyer, 2021).

But we are homo sapiens sapiens and come with the potential for mental time travel to anticipate and imagine our future and all that is needed to put it to good use.

Today there is a whole body of scientific evidence in social psychology exploring the phenomenon of future self-continuity, which supports the idea that incorporating futures thinking into your decisions, choices and actions improves your health, wellbeing, quality of life and that of others.

> "When the future self shares similarities with the present self, when it is viewed in vivid and realistic terms, and when it is seen in a positive light, people are more willing to make choices today that may benefit them at some point in the years to come." (Hershfield, 2011)

Chapter 7: Your Future Self

If you/we want a better future, you/we can make it happen. If you/we want a GREAT future, you/we have to start living with the future in mind – in other words, adopt a futures mindset.

Future self-continuity

Do unto yourself as your future self would do unto you.

Tom Meyers

Future self-continuity: had you heard of it before I mentioned the concept in the Introduction? I hadn't heard of it myself until about two weeks ago. This is what I love about writing and doing research. It's so enriching, and you never know what you'll find on the journey.

So, nearing the end of this book, I found out that what I call Futurizing Yourself has a scientific alter ego, so to speak, a.k.a. future self-continuity. This prompted me to do some re-editing of what I had already written.

As a reminder, "future self-continuity" means that, to the extent that people feel more continuity between their present and future selves, they are more likely to make decisions with the future self in mind.

Pure scientists might disagree with this, but I hope you will permit me to see some similarities between the two concepts. They both propose that thinking about your future self in positive, vivid and realistic terms is beneficial for your health and wellbeing and affects your behaviour. By contrast, not thinking about the future self at all – and leaving it all up to chance, or being in conflict with one's future self – has detrimental consequences for your health and wellbeing.

Maybe it is better to say that futurizing yourself contributes to increased future self-continuity. Anyway, for me, it proves once more that thinking about the future is not a waste of time. On the contrary: it has many benefits which contribute to making better decisions and choices for a better life that I attribute to the Futures Effect.

Remember how unhappy I was with my life, having left it up to chance and fate, and how I wanted a GREAT future. A GREAT future that is now my ongoing present – because I committed, and have been committing ever since, to my future self.

From "good for nothing" to receiving messages like this one:

> I was recommended to take my daughter to see Tom by a very good friend of mine. My daughter was suffering a lot from migraines, so I decided to book an appointment. I also booked one for myself out of curiosity and also because I discovered on his website that he combines osteopathy with stress coaching. So I said to myself, why not... I am stressed all the time, and it would be good to have a session! What a surprise! From the first visit, I immediately felt a big connection with him, like I have met this soul before, maybe in another life... I also discovered during my first session that he is the author of *Futurize Yourself – Design your life on purpose*. I bought the book and have read it three times over the past two months. The book is amazing. I found so many resemblances with my past and started to see my past in a different light.
>
> Thanks to the book and mainly thanks to Tom's own Reaset Approach, my life changed so much! I am really receptive to the way he works. Every time, after a session, I feel quiet for a couple of days, then really emotional. I brainstorm a lot to get some answers to why I am suddenly so emotional. Then after a couple of days, I get the whys.
>
> I have the impression that I have lived and progressed more

during the last four months than in all my 57 years of life. I am really grateful that my friend suggested Tom. I feel in love with life now. And by the way, my daughter also feels much better after a few sessions; the migraines have disappeared!

Thanks, Tom. I will keep coming to you, I have many things to heal, and you are the right person for helping me, and I am sure that I will soon have a healthy and fulfilled life. A life with purpose. As you said, a light that deserves to shine. Thanks so much again and again.

With gratitude, Silvia (8 February 2022)

The gratitude I felt when receiving this – as a benefit of futurizing myself – is what I want you to experience in your own way. I want you to have a GREAT future, become who you were born to be, and contribute to a better world and future for all.

For this, you need to know what the future you want, and commit to closing the gap between your future self and your present self, so you can make better long-term decisions and choices and take better actions from now on and evolve on purpose.

Chapter 7: Your Future Self

Forewarned is forearmed

The future already exists in the present, as potential.

Author unknown

Some closing thoughts as you near the end of this book. The first one is that, although your future self may feel, on a neural level, like a stranger – someone you don't care for – you can make it into your best friend by consciously linking your current self with your future self.

Another aspect to bring up again is that, with change – good or bad – your stress and anxiety levels will rise – which, if not managed in time, will change your time perception, making you more focused on the present, and will increase the likelihood of your being sick or having an accident.

Thirdly, you, just like so many of us, are laden with limiting beliefs and a short-sighted mindset that restrict you from living to your full potential. You/we are complicated beings, living in an ever more complicated, fast-changing and challenging world.

But it's not because you/we, life, the universe, is complicated that you/we can't learn to get a grip on it. Unless you don't care about certain future scenarios playing out, that is. A scenario, for example, where you/we didn't act soon enough to stop temperatures rising by more than 1.5 degrees Celsius. As a reminder, if temperatures rise by more than 1.5 degrees Celsius, more places on Earth will become uninhabitable. This will give rise to mass migration, poverty, shortage of food, declining biodiversity – and the power struggle that will ensue will provoke war.

Another doom scenario is one that probably plays out at the same time as the one I just mentioned, and where you/we realise, too late, that you/we have lost control over artificial intelligence. When this scenario plays out, what do you think will happen? I don't know what, but I can't imagine it will be anything good. Imagine a rogue AI controlling stock markets, all digital platforms, transport, nuclear power plants… Yeah, nothing good can come from that.

But we don't need to look to the horizon for examples of what we don't want. As automation, robotisation and digitisation take an ever-bigger toll on the job market, how sure is it that your job will still exist in 5 to 10 years' time?

Unlike in times gone by, where you/we needed to be reactive – fight-or-flight – to survive in the face of clear and present danger, today, with our environment changing faster than we are, being reactive is not good enough any more if we want to survive as a species. We need to be reactive and proactive in dealing with possible threats.

Reactive because, when you are standing in the middle of the road and a car is speeding your way, you still need to jump immediately. The same applies when an unexpected and unpredictable challenge comes your way. Being reactive in the face of danger (stress response) is essential for y'our survival, and the same is true for any unexpected and sudden danger.

However, just like looking left, right and in front to check there is no danger coming, we can also look ahead towards the future, anticipate possible scenarios and prepare for them – and even prevent some from happening. Proactivity, unlike reactivity, is not an autonomous response – it is done by our own volition, done on purpose.

Futurizing Yourself is proactively thinking about y'our future instead of leaving y'our fate up to chance ("Que Sera, Sera"). It is envisaging the future in order to make better long-term decisions and choices in the present that steer you in the direction of y'our preferred future. A preferred future being a future that will best suit y'our health and wellbeing and the wellbeing of the planet on which you/we depend.

I don't want to scare you here, but I'm just stating the facts, and I believe that forewarned is forearmed. Wouldn't you rather avoid pain and misery if you could? Well, I'm giving you the key to do just that. I want you to flourish in the flow of evolution and thrive in this fast-changing world. I want to empower you to navigate the changes and challenges ahead, and steer the future in the direction where you prevent unwanted scenarios from being realised because you have acted in time. Y'our health and wellbeing and y'our survival depend on it.

In truth, futurizing yourself is more a matter of empowering yourself to adapt in time and develop greater resilience to cope with the demands of tomorrow – empowering yourself, today and every day, to make decisions and choices and take action based on your future, or at least keeping your future in mind.

Rewire yourself for the future

Our very survival depends on our ability to stay awake, to adjust to new ideas, to remain vigilant and to face the challenge of change.

Martin Luther King Jr.

The benefits of futurizing yourself are innumerable, and the time spent is by no means giving up on the good things in life – quite the opposite, if my own experience is anything to go by.

This is why I am sharing my thoughts and experience with you. I do this because, yes, personally and professionally, I'm very concerned about the future of y'our health and wellbeing in this fast-changing world, and especially the current lack of consideration that is being given to how you and we all will cope with the increasing stress levels that all these changes, challenges and opportunities will bring about, while stress is already considered one of the biggest health problems worldwide.

Stress, and I see this in my practice every day, is directly or indirectly linked to neck, shoulder and back pain, heart disease, cancer, dementia, obesity and, yes, also COVID-19. But that is not all! Stress is also linked to mental health problems including anxiety and depression, insomnia, mood changes, memory problems, learning difficulties, and impaired resilience and adaptability.

Very disconcerting, too, is the fact that, over time, stress can change the size of your brain. As stress changes the blood circulation, this can actually lead to structural changes in your brain. As mentioned before, long-term stress can lead to an increased size of the amygdala. The amygdala is the key player in processing fear, thus making you more alert and anxious. Other parts of the brain, like the hippocampus and the prefrontal cortex, can actually shrink. And I do mean reduce in volume.

Knowing that the hippocampus is related to memory and the prefrontal cortex is responsible for cognition, planning, decision-making and anticipation, I'm sure that you – like me – can figure out and deduce that, when these parts become smaller and less wired, this will have consequences, for example, for your behaviour, and that thinking about the future in a constructive way – for which you need your prefrontal cortex – will become challenging, if not impossible.

Your outdated stress response, which is designed to deal with immediate problems, is very good at dealing with acute physical threats, but it hasn't evolved to deal with the new, more psychosocial and technological challenges of today, nor with future ones, and we can be sure that it isn't going to catch up and evolve fast enough for the demands of tomorrow.

This conflict means, as I see it, that the stress response has become a stressor itself, and a nuisance and something harmful to your health and wellbeing. So I hope you understand why I'm very concerned about how you will cope and deal with all the changes and challenges ahead that will, without a doubt, increase your stress levels even further.

Again, yes, I'm concerned – but I also know a solution. That solution lies with you. You have the power to make the future GREAT. You have the power within to empower yourself to evolve on purpose and become more resilient for the changes of tomorrow through your decisions, choices and actions.

A wise man once said that we cannot solve our problems with the same thinking that created them. And that is exactly what needs to happen: you need to adopt a new way to respond to the problems of tomorrow.

Human evolution has been driven to respond to immediate physical threats, but now that our environment is evolving faster than we are and the threats to our existence have changed, our body's natural reaction to danger – led by the stress response that prepares you for fight-or-flight – doesn't protect or prepare you for the challenges of tomorrow.

For the challenges of tomorrow, we need to learn, and implement on purpose, a new, more proactive stress management approach that prepares us for tomorrow's situations ahead of time by taking responsibility for our future, rather than turning a blind eye to it or waiting for things to unfold.

You have the potential to learn and develop this proactive futures mindset.

You can learn and develop it through designing your life on purpose and taking responsibility for y'our future. This means, among other things, exploring y'our future on purpose, predicting what will change or not change, creating scenarios for y'our future, envisioning what you want and don't want, and then "changing forward" by making the decisions and choices, and taking the actions needed to make the future you want into an ongoing reality.

This is what Futurizing Yourself is all about. Proactively and on purpose incorporating futures thinking into your decisions, choices and actions to "change forward" and create a GREAT future for y'ourself. Again, when I say "for y'ourself" and "y'our", I mean for you and others. Because, in our increasingly interconnected and interdependent world, your choices will also have an impact on others, and vice versa, more than ever before.

Why will this help you to evolve on purpose? Well, because the way you see the future will influence the way you act, and as you act, so you will become.

The future doesn't just happen. Unlike the past – which has come and gone – the future is always in the making and is being created "right here, right now" with every decision and choice you make and through the actions you take.

The future – your future and the future of humanity – is about human transformation, and what is needed to cope and navigate this fast-changing world is to have a proactive mindset and use y'our potential to evolve on purpose – before it is too late.

So I ask you: "What the future do you want?" Do you want to be ready for the future, the workforce of tomorrow, and ready to be able to navigate the changes ahead and have a GREAT future? A Good future... A future where you are Resilient not only in body, mind and spirit but also able to adapt and navigate all the changes ahead... A future where you Evolve and grow into the best version of yourself... An Actionable future where your actions lead you to flourish and thrive... A future that Transcends your limiting beliefs, serves the greater good and future generations.

Then set aside the limiting beliefs you might have which have stopped you from coming into your full potential. Adopt a futures mindset and make a GREAT future your priority.

Start to take time to zoom out and explore the future from a broader perspective. Ask yourself: what the future do I want? Do you want to be content, fulfilled and healthy? Do you want to have a GREAT future? Yes? Then what do you need to do in order to have all of that and more?

Create a narrative of y'our future which is based on your potential but that is agile enough to adapt to the needs of tomorrow and the years to come.

Start exploring how emerging technologies, climate change, datafication, automation and robotisation will impact you, your narrative and the people around you. Create scenarios of the future and see what you can and need to do, learn and implement, going forward, to navigate the changes and challenges ahead. And make sure to mind your body before your body reminds you! In other words: take enough time to proactively manage your health and wellbeing, which are key to your success and a GREAT future.

And remember, for now and forever: the future is built on the decisions and choices you make, the actions you take or don't take, and the time you have left to make a difference.

Yes, many aspects of y'our life are outside of your control – but you have more control over y'our life than you think.

Afterword

Your decisions, choices and actions matter. Your life matters. Make it count, and make it GREAT for yourself and others!

Tom Meyers

The Futures Effect

Futurize Yourself

You are the key to y'our future.

Tom Meyers

What do you want the future to be like? What do you aspire to achieve, be, feel, create and be remembered for?

Don't answer immediately, even if you know the answer.

> Today, we are living in a fast-changing and ever more complex and ambiguous world. A world that is trying to cope and navigate the COVID-19 pandemic and the devastating effects of climate change.
>
> At the same time, every aspect of y'our life is and will further be influenced by automation, robotisation, datafication, and so many other changes and challenges due to technological advances that have outpaced our own natural evolution.
>
> The future is a big unknown and, compared to the present, will bring even more change and uncertainty. For many, just thinking about the future can trigger anxiety, so they'd rather not think about it – which can have detrimental consequences, as an unwanted future can become a reality through one's ignorance.
>
> As you see y'our future, so you act; as you act, so you and y'our world become.

For now, just take a deep breath, close your eyes and step

Afterword

inside yourself. Slowly breathe in and out, feel within and connect with your inner being.

How do you feel? Don't think, just observe.

> Be honest with yourself, and connect with your true feelings. Are you anxious or confident about the future?

Now, imagine you are travelling to the future – to your last day on Earth – and look back. With an overview perspective, look at yourself – your life – like an astronaut would look at the Earth when they arrive in an orbit around our planet for the first time.

Look back on your life with the same awe and connection astronauts feel when they see the Earth from this cosmic perspective.

Look back at what has come and gone but also your outlook on life, your desires and aspirations. Do this without judgement but with a thankful, open heart, an open mind and curiosity.

> Are you living a good life, feeling content, fulfilled and healthy? Are you developing your potential? Are you evolving into the best version of yourself that is ready and agile enough to adapt and cope with the changes and challenges ahead? Are you being a good ancestor?

You are now a time-travelling astronaut who is looking back from the future. Observe – don't judge or use words to describe what you see. Let the feelings flow in and out at the rhythm of your breath, and let the images that emerge unfold like a film in front of your mind's eye.

Feel and observe with wonder and awe all the steps you took, the decisions and choices you made and the actions you took, and all the experiences and learnings of the years that have brought you to this, your final day on Earth.

> The past is a teacher – learn from it. The future is yet to be written, but what will it be when one day it becomes your present and that slips into a memory and turns into the past?

How do you feel viewing yourself from this future perspective? Whatever feelings come rolling over you, acknowledge them, be grateful, say "Thank you". Don't let yourself be overwhelmed by the feelings or realisations, but let them help you raise your awareness.

> You are here to become aware, evaluate and establish your " DNA for the future" based on resolute unchangeable ideals, that you can use as a guiding (G), organising (O) and development (D) principle to evolve on purpose and live a GREAT life and future. In any moment, crisis or not, to know who you are, what you can build on and what the future you want is key to weathering the many changes and challenges of this fast-changing, volatile, uncertain, complex and ambiguous world. A world full of opportunities, as the future is what you and we make of it.

Keep your eyes closed for a moment longer. With your mind's

Afterword

eye, keep looking back – but now, expand your awareness. Expand your field of vision and start seeing around you. You are not alone. You are of one with more than 8 billion souls. Souls that are having the same experience as you and, like you, are travelling on Spaceship Earth that is moving at a speed of 107,000 kilometres per hour around the Sun.

> You need to distance and reset yourself to be able to think and take stock of the situation. To think carefully about the situation or event, and consider your options, before you can decide what you need and/or want to achieve, aspire to, or create. Only then can you make the needed decisions and choices, and take the actions that matter.

You are, of one, moving together in a fast-changing and ever more complex world, as you can see from this perspective. Zoom in and you'll see that you are of one, connected through decisions, choices, actions and more. Observe and see how what you say or do influences others and how others, in turn, influence the many and shape your behaviour, as you are one. Hold on to that insight.

> There is a need for you to understand that you are not alone, never were and never will be, and that your decisions, choices and actions have an impact on others, and vice versa. How aware are you that all your decisions, choices and actions influence others? That said, every decision or choice you don't make and every action you don't take influences others too.

Now, refocus your awareness back to you and ask yourself: "If this was indeed my last day on Earth, am I content and fulfilled with what I have achieved? Was I good to myself, my health and wellbeing? Was I able to adapt and self-manage myself in what has become a fast-changing world? Was my life meaningful? Did I become a better person? And now, leaving this world, am I leaving it a better place than it was when I entered it? Will I be considered a good ancestor?"

> You are an "organisation" of trillions of cells that – just like organisations we have created – live with and for others, compete with others and need others to survive. We live in that same fast-changing world, in which we also want to be relevant and succeed. So, just like organisations, we need to anticipate possible, plausible, probable or preferable scenarios of the future, and then take action in order to prepare ourselves ahead of change. We – and that means each and every one of us, including you – need to think about y'our role in the future and prepare y'ourself for when the future becomes the present. It will save you a lot of stress and harm to your health and wellbeing, and that of the people around you.

What say you?

> At a basic level, we all want the same thing. We all want to have a good life, where we are resilient and evolve into the best version of ourselves. We want to act with meaning and

purpose, and avoid pain. We want to leave this life knowing that we have left the world a better place for our being in it. We want to be good ancestors. In other words, we want to have a GREAT life – a GREAT future.

Would others be of one mind with you? Or…

Think about what the future you want, and treat it as the present. Think about uniting possible, plausible, probable, preferable and projected futures for the good of mankind.

In order to flourish and thrive, there is a need to incorporate futures thinking into all your decisions, choices and actions on purpose. There is also a need to think ahead about not only what you want, but what we need. You are simultaneously a whole in and of itself, as well as a part of a larger whole. This means that, as a human being, you are both a part and the whole of humanity.

It's time to go back, until we meet again.

But before you go, tell me: What do you want your future to be like? Or, as I like to put it: What "the future" do you want?

The future is screaming for y'our attention. We need new narratives for the future. Will you write yours? Will you design the future you want to see and evolve into on purpose? Will you, like so many others around the world, adopt a futures mindset and act purposefully today to change the course of y'our future – and make it one that future generations will thank you for? Or will you stay on the sidelines and turn a blind eye ("Que Sera, Sera")?

It is time…

It's time to wake up to y'our full potential and design your life on purpose. It's time to make the decisions, time to make the choices, and time to take the actions that are urgently needed – to create a GREAT future for you personally and for us all.

Be good to you and y'our future, always!

Tom

Afterword

To be continued...

The Futures Effect

ADDENDUM

DON'T start with why!

Tom Meyers, 26 March 2020

Why is not the first question any more, but what is?

I'm not sure if you've seen Simon Sinek's TED talk "How great leaders inspire action". Yes, the video with more than 40 million views about the Golden Circle, better known as the video on "Start with Why".

In this video, Simon Sinek explains how he codified "how" and "why" inspiring leaders and organisations in the world to act and communicate in completely the opposite way to everyone else. They start communicating with "why they do it" first instead of "what they do and how". By "why" he means: "Their purpose; cause; belief. Why they exist. Why they get out of bed in the morning."

He also relates that this is all grounded in the tenets of biology. Simplistically explained, our neocortex, the outer and newest layer of the brain, is responsible for rational and analytical thought and language, corresponding with the WHAT level, and the limbic or middle brain is responsible for emotional and motivational processes and feelings, like trust and loyalty, corresponding with the WHY and HOW. The reptile brain is the instinctual brain that doesn't ask questions; it just reacts.

In his book *Find Your Why* (2017), I read: "Once you understand your WHY, you'll be able to clearly articulate what makes you feel fulfilled and to better understand what drives your behaviour when you're at your natural best. When you can do that, you'll have a point of reference for everything you do going forward. You'll be able to make more intentional choices for your business, your career and your life. You'll be able to inspire others to buy from you, work with you and join your cause."

Before I start questioning what is written there, I want to say, yes, I believe from personal experience, and it has been proven by science over and over again, that having a purpose gives a point of reference for everything you do going forward – and not only when you're at your natural best. It gives you resilience in challenging time, and in moments like today (forced to stay at home due to COVID-19), it gives me, at least, an anchor with which I can adapt more easily to the new situation.

But something bothers me with this "start with why". First of all, it's very rigid… it is portrayed (or am I perceiving it wrongly?) as "this is the way it is done, and no other way". Secondly, it seems very much based on a behaviour that is outdated and controlling. Simon Sinek comes from the advertising industry, so his background is about how to influence our emotions. In his book, he says it himself: "Leading with why has a deeper, more emotional and ultimately more influential value" – and remember, the title of his talk is "How great leaders inspire action".

So "WHY" talks to our emotions, and our emotions are coloured through our past experiences, culture and so many other factors. Today, we also live in an era where many people live predominantly on fear-based emotions… Fear is an emotion induced by perceived danger or threat (COVID-19, emerging technologies taking jobs…). Fear causes physiological changes and ultimately behavioural changes, such as fleeing, hiding, freezing, but also panic-buying tons of toilet paper and pasta. Fear is not about others; it is about the individual…

So, now I'm thinking in terms of the concept "Evolving on Purpose". Evolving on purpose meaning deliberately participating in your evolution, which requires a more distant and integrative long-term view on your life. These specific faculties are related to the neocortex – that part of the brain involved in higher-order brain functions such as perception, cognition, spatial reasoning, visualisation and long-term projection.

So, in this concept, if "why" is related to the limbic brain, it is NOT the question we want to ask first. The first question becomes "WHAT"… This "WHAT" is specific and should not be based on our emotions.

So, when I look back at Simon Sinek's Golden Circle, I see another circle emerging that goes beyond the model and folds itself in and around it.

So instead of starting with "why", you can start with "what" and then ask "why" to reinforce it!

Ask yourself: "On an ideal day, what do I want to feel?" – and I do mean "what", not "how" you're feeling, because then we're back at the limbic system, according to Simon Sinek's model.

Your response:

My response is: "No matter the situation, at any moment in my life I want to feel content, fulfilled and healthy."

Question: How many of the feelings I mentioned do you want to feel too?

Now, stretch your imagination a bit. Can you imagine that everyone wants to feel this way? I can.

So now, coming from a future holistic overview perspective, what can YOU do that no one else can do to make this feeling a reality – and HOW?

Why? Because you want that feeling (in another article, I'll write about why you need to differentiate feelings from emotions) which is associated with your potential and being in your element in the collective.

If we want to evolve on purpose – meaning, with volition – when we want to transcend our outdated programming, we have to start reasoning from a different perspective. A future perspective that we evolve into is a scenario that I'm participating in.

The Futures Effect

Change Your Story, Change Y'our Future!

RESOURCES

You can find free downloads and more information about Tom, his writing, talks, various courses and osteopathy practice on:

Websites	www.futurizeyourself.com
	www.meyerstom.com
	www.osteopathbrussels.com
LinkedIn	www.linkedin.com/in/meyerstom
Facebook	www.facebook.com/futurizeyourself

Want to have a meaningful conversation with Tom, invite him to speak or give a workshop at your next event?

Contact	info@futurizeyourself.com
More information	www.thefutureseffect.com

RECOMMENDED BOOKS

REFERENCES

APA Dictionary of Psychology. *Life Change Units.* https://dictionary.apa.org/life-change-units

Arnsten, A. (2009). Stress signalling pathways that impair prefrontal cortex structure and function. *Nature Reviews Neuroscience,* 10, 410–422. https://doi.org/10.1038/nrn2648

Aten, J. (2020). *Jeff Bezos on Planning for the Future in Uncertain Times.* INC. https://www.inc.com/jason-aten/with-this-simple-3-word-question-jeff-bezos-explains-how-to-plan-for-future-despite-turbulent-times.html

Ayduk, Ö. and Kross, E. (2010). From a distance: Implications of spontaneous self-distancing for adaptive self-reflection. *Journal of Personality and Social Psychology,* 98 (5), 809–829.

Barabasi, A. (2014). *Linked: How Everything Is Connected to Everything Else and What It Means for Business, Science, and Everyday Life.* Basic Books; Illustrated edition.

Blechschmidt, E. (2004) *The Ontogenetic basis of human anatomy. A biodynamic approach to development from conception to birth.* Pacific Distributing.

Brietzke, S., and Meyer, M. L. (2021). Temporal self-compression: Behavioral and neural evidence that past and future selves are compressed as they move away from the present. *PNAS Proceedings of the National Academy of Sciences of the United States of America,* 118(49), Article e2101403118. https://doi.org/10.1073/pnas.2101403118

Clark, S. (2021). *German astronaut to become 600th person to fly into space.* Spaceflight Now. https://spaceflightnow.com/2021/10/27/german-astronaut-to-become-600th-person-to-fly-into-space

Conway, M. (2014). *A thinking futures reference guide. Foresight: an introduction.* http://choo.ischool.utoronto.ca/fis/courses/inf1005/foresight.intro.conway.pdf

Damasio, A. (2018). *The Strange Order of Things: Life, Feeling, and the Making of Cultures.* Pantheon.

Derouin, S. (2021). Antarctic Study Shows How Much Space Dust Hits Earth Every Year. *Scientific American.* https://www.scientificamerican.com/article/antarctic-study-shows-how-much-space-dust-hits-earth-every-year

Dispenza, J. (2019). *Change the Box, Change Your Reality: Part III*. Dr Joe Dispenza. https://drjoedispenza.com/blogs/dr-joes-blog/change-your-box-change-your-reality-part-iii

Draudt, A. and West, J.R. (2016). *What the Foresight: Your personal futures explored. Defy the expected and define the preferred*. CreateSpace Independent Publishing Platform.

Figueres, C. and Rivett-Carnac, T. (2020). *The Future We Choose*. Knopf.

Frankl, V. (2006). *Man's Search for Meaning*. Beacon Press.

Ganschow, B., Cornet, L., Zebel, S., and van Gelder, J. (2021). Looking Back From the Future: Perspective Taking in Virtual Reality Increases Future Self-Continuity. *Frontiers in Psychology*, 12. https://doi.org/10.3389/fpsyg.2021.664687

Gendlin, E. (1966). *The discovery of felt meaning*. In J.B. McDonald & R.R. Leeper (Eds.), Language and meaning. Papers from the ASCD Conference, The Curriculum Research Institute (Nov. 21–24, 1964 & March 20–23, 1965), pp. 45–62. Washington, DC: Association for Supervision and Curriculum Development. From http://previous.focusing.org/gendlin/docs/gol_2039.html

Gilbert, D. (2006). *Humans Wired to Respond to Short-Term Problems*. NPR. https://www.npr.org/templates/story/story.php?storyId=5530483&t=1636527859778

Green, J. (2014). *The Fault in Our Stars*. Penguin Books.

Grupe, D., and Nitschke, J. (2013). Uncertainty and anticipation in anxiety: an integrated neurobiological and psychological perspective. *Nature Reviews Neuroscience*, 14(7), 488–501. https://doi.org/10.1038/nrn3524

Hallbom, K. and Hallbom, T. (2012). *Exploring the Neuroscience and Magic Behind Setting Your Intent – And Creating an Optimal Future for Yourself*. NLPCA https://nlpca.com/creating-an-optimal-future-for-yourself

Hershfield, H. (2011). Future self-continuity: how conceptions of the future self transform intertemporal choice. *Annals of the New York Academy of Sciences*, 1235, 30-43. https://doi.org/10.1111/j.1749-6632.2011.06201.x

IMCI (2022). *International Market & Competitive Intelligence Magazine*. January/February. https://www.flipsnack.com/imcimagazine/imci-magazine-january-february-2022

IPCC (2021). *Climate Change 2021: The Physical Science Basis*. Cambridge University Press.

Jackson Curran, E. (2020). *Here's why planning a trip can help your mental health*. National Geographic. https://www.nationalgeographic.com/travel/article/planning-a-trip-is-good-for-you-especially-during-pandemic

Johnson, B. (2020). *Mindshift #2: Think "now, future, next."* Forbes. https://www.forbes.com/sites/amberjohnson-jimludema/2020/11/09/beyond-covid-19-three-mindshift-strategies-to-chart-a-clear-path-forward/?sh=5c3ac3e07cbf

Johnson, B. (2021). *The Future You*. HarperOne.

Kirmmse, B. (2008). *Kierkegaard's Journals and Notebooks*, Volume 2, Journals EE-KK, Princeton University Press.

Koestler, A. (1982). *The Ghost in the Machine*. One 70 Press.

Krznaric, R. (2021). *The Good Ancestor: A Radical Prescription for Long-Term Thinking*. The Experiment.

Levi, Y. and Freedland, J. (2021). *A Conversation - with special guest Yuval Noah Harari.* Unholy. https://omny.fm/shows/unholy/a-conversation-with-special-guest-yuval-noah-harar

Leonard, G. (2021). *Fork in the Road Project: The Manifesto*. https://forkintheroadmanifesto.wordpress.com/manifesto

Lewis, J. (2012). *A T. Still: From the Dry Bone to the Living Man*. Dry Bone Press.

Lombardo, T. (2017). *Future Consciousness: The Path to Purposeful Evolution*. Changemakers Books.

Marantz Henig, R. (2020). *Experts warned of a pandemic decades ago. Why weren't we ready?* National Geographic. https://www.nationalgeographic.com/science/article/experts-warned-pandemic-decades-ago-why-not-ready-for-coronavirus

Maslin, M. (2021). *How To Save Our Planet: The Facts*. Penguin Life.

McCullough, E. (2019). *Rising sea levels threaten the Belgian coast*. The Brussels Times. https://www.brusselstimes.com/belgium/69902/rising-sea-levels-threaten-the-belgian-coast

McGonigal, J. (2017). *Our Puny Human Brains Are Terrible at Thinking About the Future*. Slate. https://slate.com/technology/2017/04/why-people-are-so-bad-at-thinking-about-the-future.html

Meyers, T. (2018). *Futurize Yourself – Design your life on purpose*. Filament Publishing.

Meyers, T. (2020). *Feel it on purpose*. Personal blog. https://meyerstom.wordpress.com/2020/03/27/feel-it-on-purpose

Mishra, T., Wang, M., Metwally, A.A. et al. (2020). Pre-symptomatic detection of COVID-19 from smartwatch data. *Nature Biomedical Engineering*, 4, 1208–1220. https://doi.org/10.1038/s41551-020-00640-6

Mitchell, E. (2008). *The Way of the Explorer: An Apollo Astronaut's Journey Through the Material and Mystical Worlds, Revised Edition*. Weiser.

Murray, S., et al. (2004). Exploring the spiritual needs of people dying of lung cancer or heart failure: a prospective qualitative interview study of patients and their carers. *Palliative Medicine*, 18(1), 39–45. https://doi.org/10.1191/0269216304pm837oa

NPR (2013). *Resetting the Theory of Time*. NPR. https://www.npr.org/2013/05/17/184775924/resetting-the-theory-of-time?t=1637399672656

Oyserman, D. (2009). Identity-based motivation: Implications for action-readiness, procedural-readiness, and consumer behavior. *Journal of Consumer Psychology*, 19(3), 250–260. https://doi.org/10.1016/j.jcps.2009.05.008

Polk, M., et al. (2020). Thinking ahead and staying in the present: Implications for reactivity to daily stressors. *Personality and Individual Differences* 161. https://doi.org/10.1016/j.paid.2020.109971

Porges, S. (2011). *The Polyvagal Theory: Neurophysiological Foundations of Emotions, Attachment, Communication, and Self-regulation*. W. W. Norton & Company.

Prince William (2019). *The Earthshot Prize*. https://earthshotprize.org

Rosenberg, S. (2017). *Accessing the Healing Power of the Vagus Nerve: Self-Help Exercises for Anxiety, Depression, Trauma, and Autism*. North Atlantic Books.

Rushkoff, D. (2018). *Why Futurists Suck*. Nesta's FutureFest. https://youtu.be/uEYPziegNgg

Rutchick, A. et al. (2018) Future Self-Continuity Is Associated With Improved Health and Increases Exercise Behavior. *Journal of Experimental Psychology: Applied*, 24(1), 72–80. https://doi.org/10.1037/xap0000153

Schwab, K. and Malleret, T. (2021). *The Great Narrative*. Schweizer Buchhändler und Verleger-Verband SBVV.

Scientific American Mind (2005). *Feeling Our Emotions*. Scientific American. https://www.scientificamerican.com/article/feeling-our-emotions

Sinek, S. (2017). *Find Your Why: A Practical Guide for Discovering Purpose for You and Your Team*. Portfolio.

Smolin, L. (2014). *Time Reborn: From the Crisis in Physics to the Future of the Universe*. Penguin Book Ltd.

Stansberry, K., et al. (2019). *Experts Optimistic About the Next 50 Years of Digital Life. Chapter 3: Humanity is at a precipice; its future is at stake*. PEW Research Centre. https://www.pewresearch.org/internet/2019/10/28/3-humanity-is-at-a-precipice-its-future-is-at-stake

Sterling P. (2012). Allostasis: a model of predictive regulation. *Physiology & Behavior*, 106(1), 5–15. https://doi.org/10.1016/j.physbeh.2011.06.004

Sterling, P., Eyer, J. (1988): *Allostasis: A new paradigm to explain arousal pathology*. In Fisher S, Reason J, (eds), Handbook of Life Stress, Cognition and Health. John Wiley & Sons.

Still, A.T. (1908). *Autobiography of Andrew T. Still*. Published by the author. Available at https://archive.lib.msu.edu/DMC/Osteopathy/autobiographystill1908.pdf

Suddendorf, T., et al. (2016). *Shaping one's future self: The development of deliberate practice*. In K. Michaelian, S. B. Klein, & K. K. Szpunar (Eds.), Seeing the future: Theoretical perspectives on future-oriented mental time travel (pp. 343–366). Oxford University Press. https://doi.org/10.1093/acprof:oso/9780190241537.003.0017

Tavernier, L. (2022). *The Science Behind NASA's First Attempt at Redirecting an Asteroid*. NASA. https://www.jpl.nasa.gov/edu/news/2022/9/22/the-science-behind-nasas-first-attempt-at-redirecting-an-asteroid

Thiel, P. (2014). *Zero to One: Notes on Start Ups, or How to Build the Future*. Crown Business.

Uyeda, J., Hansen, T., Arnold, S., & Pienaar, J. (2011). The million-year wait for macroevolutionary bursts. *Proceedings of the National Academy of*

Sciences of the United States of America, 108(38), 15908–15913. https://doi.org/10.1073/pnas.1014503108

Vilhauer, J. (2014). *Think Forward to Thrive*. New World Library.

Voski, A. (2020). The ecological significance of the overview effect: Environmental attitudes and behaviours in astronauts. *Journal of Environmental Psychology* 70, 101454. https://doi.org/10.1016/j.jenvp.2020.101454

WEF (2019). *What if we get things right? Visions for 2030*. WEF. https://www.weforum.org/agenda/2019/10/future-predictions-what-if-get-things-right-visions-for-2030

WEF (2020). *We need a global reskilling revolution – here's why*. WEF. https://www.weforum.org/agenda/2020/01/reskilling-revolution-jobs-future-skills

WEF (2022). *Reskilling Revolution: Preparing 1 billion people for tomorrow's economy*. WEF. https://www.weforum.org/impact/reskilling-revolution

WEF (2022). *The space economy is booming. What benefits can it bring to Earth?* WEF. https://www.weforum.org/agenda/2022/10/space-economy-industry-benefits

Wetli, P. (2020). *'Earthrise,' The Photo That Propelled the Environmental Movement and Led to Earth Day*. WTTW. https://news.wttw.com/2020/04/22/earthrise-photo-propelled-environmental-movement-and-led-earth-day

Wheelwright, V. (2012). *It's YOUR Future... Make it a Good One!* Personal Futures Network.

White, F. (2019). *The Cosma Hypothesis: Implications of the Overview Effect*. Independently published.

Wilson, D., Hayes, S., Biglan, A., & Embry, D. (2014). Evolving the future: Toward a science of intentional change. *Behavioral and Brain Sciences*, 37(4), 395–416. https://doi.org/10.1017/s0140525x13001593

Woebot Health. https://woebothealth.com

WWF (2019). *Un milliard de personnes menacées par le changement climatique sur les océans, les régions polaires et les montagnes, avertit un rapport de l'ONU*. WWF. https://wwf.be/fr/communiques-de-presse/un-milliard-de-personnes-menacees-par-le-changement-climatique-sur-les-oceans

The Futures Effect

The best way to ensure a great future is to create it on purpose, today.

www.futurizeyourself.com

www.ingramcontent.com/pod-product-compliance
Lightning Source LLC
LaVergne TN
LVHW020409070526
838199LV00054B/3572